◆ THEORY AND PRACTICE ◆

Engaging Readers & Writers With Inquiry

Promoting Deep Understandings in Language Arts
and the Content Areas With Guiding Questions

Jeffrey D. Wilhelm

New York • Toronto • London • Auckland • Sydney
Mexico City • New Delhi • Hong Kong • Buenos Aires

Dedication

I dedicate this book to the Lyle family,
especially Gene and Doris,
who always took their students seriously and encouraged me
to ask my own questions about serious issues.
To Paul Friedemann, with whom I learned how to use inquiry
and questioning as the framing purpose of teaching,
and to Brian Ambrosius, who is always asking questions,
particularly of me (for some reason!).

Cover design by Maria Lilja
Cover photos: (clockwise from top right) Dex/Getty Images,
Photodisc/GettyImages, and Blend Images/Veer.
Interior design by Solutions by Design, Inc.

ISBN-13: 978-0-439-57413-6 • ISBN-10: 0-439-57413-7

Printed in U.S.A.

9 10 40 14 15 16 17/0

TABLE OF CONTENTS

Foreword: Living the Questions

The question I ask myself most often is, "What is the problem for which *x* is the solution?" *X* might be an instructional technique or a book, a computer or a graphic organizer, any one of which I might choose to help me solve an instructional problem. More and more kids ask this question, at least in their minds, wondering what is the problem for which school is the solution. For many, too many, it has become a place they go to learn skills in the name of standards and state tests; real learning, however, is always more intentional, taking place in a context rich in purpose and personal meaning. To return to my question: What is the problem for which this book is the solution? It is the problem of providing a rich curriculum for all students, one guided by the questions they need answers to and the questions such a curriculum will teach them to ask. Such a curriculum teaches students, as the poet Rainer Maria Rilke said, to "live the questions." This is what Jeff Wilhelm asks his readers to do here and to give students a chance to do, as well.

Jeff offers us all an important resource to help us better understand what "inquiry" means and, more to the point, how and why we should make it the guiding principle in our teaching. Jeff also offers teachers something hard to come by: the professor's understanding of theory combined with the teacher's gift for applying those theories into practice in the classroom. This blend of theory and practice is the inevitable result of the way he works, alternating between teaching at a university one semester and in the schools the next. When he speaks of the role of inquiry, then, he does so as one who routinely faces a class of American public school students who wonder why they should possibly read, for example, *Romeo and Juliet.* Throughout this excellent book he answers that question—for those students and for us, the teachers who must teach such texts to seemingly indifferent adolescents.

Some years ago Sam Intrator, author of *Tuned in and Fired Up: How Teaching Can Inspire Real Learning in the Classroom* (2003), spent the year sitting in the back of my classroom, guided in his own inquiry by the questions: When do students engage with their learning—and why? In short, he found "when we put the brakes on the world as it rushes by, we can have a 'slow experience,' by which [he] means attending to our environment with awareness and care. Slow experience is concerned with process rather than productivity. Its end is engrossment" (30). More recently Alfred Tatum, in his book *Teaching Reading to Black Adolescent Males: Closing the Achievement Gap* (2005), emphasizes a similar theme of slowing down and making room for deeper, slower learning. "As long as the focus [of the secondary curriculum] is on increasing test scores—something that is irrelevant to many of these young men—to the exclusion of the more significant factors . . . black males will continue to struggle" (35). Tatum goes on to identify "multiple literacies" as the core of a more meaningful, effective curriculum: academic, cultural, social, and emotional.

Throughout this book by Jeff Wilhelm, you see what these multiple literacies look like in practice and learn the theories behind them. Jeff's groundbreaking work (with Michael Smith) on the literacy of adolescent boys informs this work but his message is that *all* kids, boys and girls, struggling students and high achievers, need the questions this book teaches us to ask when we read, write, or engage in class discussions. Researchers find that inquiry-based instruction consistently achieves greater personal engagement, improved academic performance, a deeper understanding, and more enduring place in students' memory than lectures and drills.

I have known Jeff Wilhelm and presented with him at NCTE for the last five years and am always impressed by the rigor of his thinking and the quality of his ideas. He is a committed researcher, one guided by his own profound inquiries; he is also one of us, a classroom teacher, who uses the ideas he shares in this book to help his students do what we ourselves try to do: to learn and love the learning along the way as we teach them to "live the questions."

—Jim Burke
San Francisco, CA

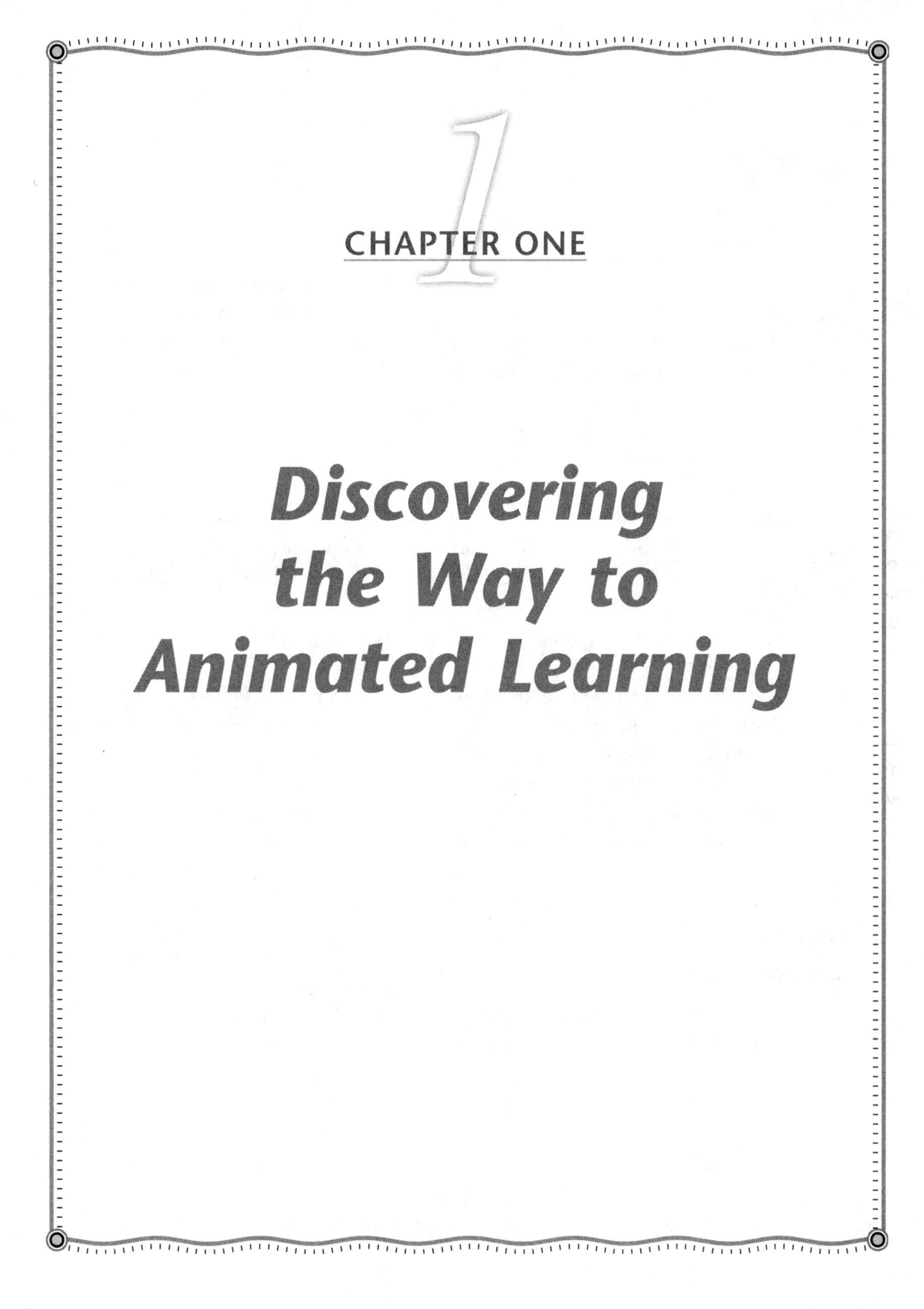

CHAPTER ONE

Discovering the Way to Animated Learning

Would your students be more excited to read *Romeo and Juliet* and hear your commentary on it or read it in the context of pursuing the question, *What makes good relationships and what screws up relationships?* Would they rather read the textbook chapter on the civil rights movement or consider what civil rights are, and how to best protect and promote them? (Have you ever met a student who *didn't* think his civil rights were being violated in some way?) Might students develop interest in questions like *What's wrong with our school and how can we improve it? How can we best provide for the needy? Why do organisms die? Is it ever okay to lie? Can the needs for security and freedom be balanced? Is it ever permissible to resist established governance?*

These are all examples of what are known variously as big questions, essential questions, or guiding questions. They can reframe what we already do in school and make it matter to students by generating a real purpose for content and students' personal connections to that curricular material. The power of guiding questions lies primarily in the power of purpose. Cognitive science has demonstrated that one's purpose drives motivation and what one attends to, remembers, and then applies. Without purpose, significant learning is difficult if not impossible to achieve.

Before I used guiding questions, my students would often ask, "Why do we have to do this stuff?" But they don't anymore. Now they know *why* we do what we do. Guiding questions create a clearly focused problem orientation for our studies that connects kids to socially significant material and learning. This in turn leads to exciting conversations that bring together the students' lives, the course content, and the world in which we live as we consolidate major concepts, vocabulary, strategies, and ideas. Now, everything we do, including class discussions and the use of questioning strategies, is in the service of addressing the guiding question. As a result, we gain a deep understanding of enduring concepts, something that is rarely achieved in school (see, e.g., Brown, Collins, & DuGuid, 1989; Tyler, 1949).

Without purpose, significant learning is difficult if not impossible to achieve.

By recasting a curricular topic in terms of a guiding question, we set the stage for a model of teaching known as "inquiry" (see Jacobs, 1989; Smith & Wilhelm, 2006; Travers, 1998; Wiggins & McTighe, 2003). The inquiry process explores and addresses the real-world problem articulated by the question. It gets at the central reasons that the material being studied was developed or discovered in the first place. It foregrounds the functionality of what is being learned.

In schools today, teachers typically "cover" the curriculum by using textbooks and lectures. This information-transmission approach, called the "curriculum-centered" model by cognitive scientists, has been discredited through the rigorous studies of Ralph Tyler (1949) and by the last thirty-plus years of research in the areas of cognition, education and literacy. The inquiry approach is a powerful alternative supported by current research. It "uncovers" the same curricular content by putting students in the position of operating on and interpreting the required material.

"He who questions much, does and discusses much, shall learn much."
—Sir Francis Bacon

The use of guiding questions connects students to real expertise as practiced in the world. Everything taught in an inquiry unit, including all attitudes, strategies, and concepts, is in the service of investigating the question, and understanding and doing things related to the question. Guiding questions provide "curricular coherence" (Applebee, et al., 2000) because all work relates to a clear central purpose, makes students active participants in disciplinary conversations, and suggests meaningful activities, writing, and culminating projects. This approach also makes clear that simply memorizing information, as we often do in school, is not sufficient. Rather, we must develop the ability to apply what we know in our investigations and in the end develop a deep understanding of the issue. After all, if we are not teaching kids how to understand and how to apply what they know, what is it that we are really teaching? If we are not teaching for these purposes, then we are simply "doing school."

When I walk around schools, I often see teachers lecturing and kids sitting silently at their desks, twirling pencils, looking dazed, and sometimes even sleeping. The only one posing questions is the teacher, and the questions are often fill-in-the-blank in spirit, designed to see if students "get" the information correctly. There is no engaging conversation that addresses a pressing problem or debatable question.

No one wants to come home from school not having spoken or substantively engaged with others or with important ideas. John Goodlad notes in *A Place Called School* (1984) that kids like shop, gym, and art classes because of the task orientation, social engagement, and informal talk that accompanies activity in these classes. Why are these qualities so absent from our content-area classes?

The work of academic disciplines is inquiry. And the most recent research in cognition shows that reading and writing are forms of inquiry, and are best learned in contexts of inquiry (Hillocks, 1999, 2002) and through the questioning and discourse that is central to it. As John Dewey and James Britton have asserted, learning floats on a sea of talk. That means that students must be the ones asking the majority of questions and doing the bulk of classroom talk. They must shake off the passive role of receiving information and become apprentices who actually do the work of the disciplines they are studying.

What Inquiry Is

This book will focus on how to create powerful classroom interactions and learning through the use of inquiry. I define inquiry, on the unit level, as the process of addressing problems expressed by guiding questions. Such big, underlying questions define and drive the activity of what cognitive scientists call "communities of practice." For example, biologists are a group defined by their pursuit of guiding questions such as "How are organisms similar and different?" or "Why do organisms die?" They are also defined by the ways they go about answering these questions: observing the natural world, forming hypotheses, collecting data to confirm or disconfirm their hypotheses, and so forth.

Through inquiry, students learn how to use heuristics—accepted problem-solving tools to construct understandings. They engage in the same kind of processes and dialogues that practitioners do, and make use of the same tools as well. They are inducted as apprentices into the ways experts know and do things.

Inquiry can also be pursued on a lesson level, as students engage in activities or discussions around an organizing question or problem important in the world.

The E's of Inquiry

Topical Inquiry . . .

- Engages with a disciplinary question
- Explores what is already known and thought
- Explains and interprets the established data, articulates connections seen in that data

Critical Inquiry . . .

- Elaborates and invents—makes new connections, fills gaps by providing new data and insights to what is already known
- Extends and applies—extrapolates what has been learned and finds applications for what has been learned
- Evaluates and adapts—reflects on and uses what has been learned in new ways and in new situations, transferring, adapting, and revising understandings as this is done

The Correspondence Conception

Cognitive scientists define inquiry as the process of accessing, building, extending, and using knowledge consistent with what is thought and known in a discipline. Students' understanding is measured in terms of the correspondence between how they know and use the concepts and strategies under study and how experts do. This is known as the "correspondence conception" (Bereiter, 2004). As Nickerson (1985) explains: "One understands a concept, principle, process or whatever to the extent that what is in one's head regarding that concept corresponds to what is in the head of an expert in the relevant field" (p. 222). Doing work sheets, for example, cannot be considered inquiry because it does not provide the context, simulate, nor profoundly challenge and change student behavior and thinking as it moves students closer to how expert readers deal with text, or how actual mathematicians deal with numbers.

The goal of teaching and learning is understanding. Understanding has several facets, described by Wiggins and McTighe (1998, 2003).

Facets of Understanding (from Wiggins & McTighe, 1998, 2003)

Facet	**Those who understand can . . .**
Facet One: Explanation	Provide thorough and verifiable accounts of phenomena and other data from the studied material.
Facet Two: Interpretation	See patterns across data related to the topic; see and articulate new connections. They can translate what they know, offer new and personal dimensions, and make what they know accessible to others.
Facet Three: Application	Powerfully use, transfer, and adapt what is known in a variety of contexts.
Facet Four: Perspective	Critically perceive and respect multiple points of view regarding the topic, and understand how competing views weigh in.
Facet Five: Empathy	Respect and find value in what is foreign and unique. They will work to understand the personal dimensions and importance of various knowledge constructions for different groups.
Facet Six: Self-Knowledge	Possess the ability to reflect on, consider, critique and revise their own thinking. They recognize how they understand and what they do and do not understand. They perceive the personal biases of themselves and others that can impede understanding. They can articulate the back story—the justification for understanding in the way they do.

A Comparison of Two Inquiry Approaches	
Understanding by Design Wiggins & McTighe, 2003	**Inquiry and Design** Lehrer et al., 1993; Wilhelm and Friedemann, 1998
W Where are we going? Why? Identify final projects	Frame the inquiry: Set goals Articulate the purpose and importance of the inquiry to student and in world Negotiate final projects Set up the backwards plan
H Hook Ask essential questions Frontload by connecting students personally to the topic	Motivate, ask guiding question Frontload, activate prior knowledge Establish personal connections to the topic
E Experience and equip students with concepts and strategies through an instructional sequence	Uncover the curriculum (topical research) Develop established conceptual and strategic tools through an instructional sequence Develop new concepts and tools (critical inquiry) through an instructional sequence
R Reflect, rethink, rehearse, revise	Analyze available data, both previously established (topical research) and that developed by students (critical inquiry) Organize the data into patterns Design and represent demonstrations of understanding into a knowledge artifact for sharing and use Present to peers, critique, rethink and revise
E Exhibit and evaluate	Re-present publicly and use for real purposes Move towards new applications and social actions

Inquiry has many models of implementation: inquiry and design, understanding by design, expeditionary learning, cognitively guided instruction in math, physics by inquiry, ChemCom, to name a few. All share the general features described in the chart above.

What Inquiry Is Not

One problem with the term *inquiry* is that it can carry associations of unwieldy, time-consuming, student-centered projects that collapse despite good intentions. My editor winced when I first proposed this book, recalling how in seventh grade she and her classmates hauled mud up from a creek near her school "for days" and then spent many more days of school time lolling on the

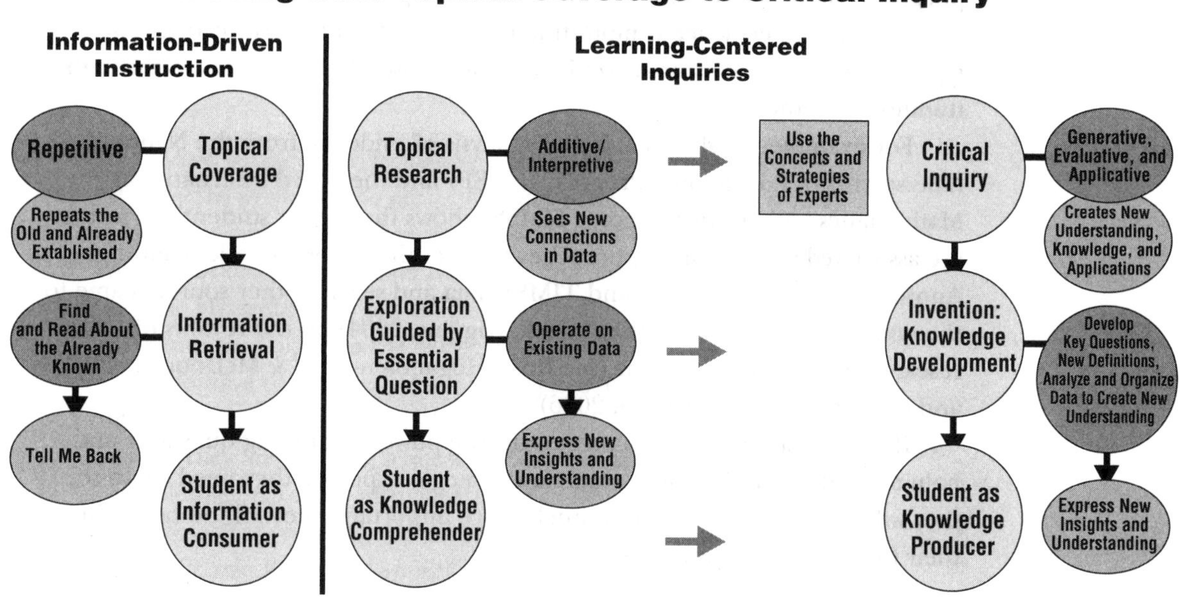

soccer field while her teacher and her teacher's compliant husband led an "inquiry" project—building a log cabin from scratch. (The teacher wound up divorced, and my editor's understanding of early America didn't progress beyond mud and straw and logs.)

Student-centered projects aren't inquiry. Nor is inquiry synonymous with a student-generated curriculum, wherein students are completely in the driver's seat. To qualify as inquiry, a project must build upon and apply disciplinary understanding. So, for example, if students create dioramas in such a way that they more fully understand how mapmaking works, they are being apprenticed into cartography, and the project can be considered a form of inquiry. If building a log cabin is conceived of as fostering a more expert understanding of architecture, strength of materials, and what architects must know and do, and students can articulate what they have learned in these terms, then it's inquiry. Otherwise, it is just "doing school," a form of what kids call "busywork" (Smith & Wilhelm, 2002).

You Can Have Your Cake and Eat It Too!

In schools we often skim across the surface of various topics in ways that bore students and teachers. In contrast, inquiry classrooms are animated and they produce results: Students and teachers address the same required content but go far beyond "coverage" to achieve deeper understanding and to learn

beliefs, desires and interests that energize the hard work of becoming literate. From this perspective, motivations and social interactions are equal to cognitions as foundations for literacy." According to literacy researcher Marty Nystrand, learning to think requires question posing, effective interaction, and real dialogue among multiple perspectives (1997). These essential processes are rarely developed in schools, as we will see, but they easily could be, through the use of inquiry approaches at the lesson or unit level.

Engaged readers converse with an author, characters, significant ideas, and one another. These conversations can lead them to think or act differently. Such readers, like all real-world practitioners, adapt and apply what they have learned. They are, like biologists, part of a community of practice. They ask compelling guiding questions about their lives and build and apply knowledge in response. They are inquirers.

This book will explain how you can help students undertake inquiry both on the unit level, through the use of guiding questions, and on the individual lesson level, through the use of questioning and discussion strategies. The research base is clear: inquiry-oriented classrooms cultivate motivation and engagement, deeper conceptual and strategic understanding, higher-level thinking, productive habits of mind, and positive attitudes toward future learning, no matter the subject area.

In the next section, I explore the problems caused by traditional approaches, inquiry as a proposed reform, and some possible reasons why this approach has not been embraced as it should be.

The 3S + 6Ms = Guidelines for Inquiry

Want a handy heuristic for remembering the process of inquiry-based teaching? The teachers with whom I work find the following super helpful when planning learning-centered teaching for understanding:

1. Set Up.
   Motivate with essential question and frontloading; personally connect kids to the content.
2. Set significant stopping points.
   Map out experiences that tap multiple modalities and measures.
   Provide multiple ways for students to learn and demonstrate their grasp of the standards/end goals/enduring understandings through various classroom activities and independent culminating projects.
3. Sequence in order to scaffold.
   Model: work *for* students: Teacher does/students watch.
   Mentor: work *with* students: Teacher does/students help and students do together/teacher helps.
   Monitor: work *by* students: Student does/teacher assesses and helps as needed.

THE BACK STORY

Is the Sky Falling? The Literacy Crisis

Despite the best intentions and funding being poured into schools, despite the tremendous energy put into implementing standards and accountability testing in order to make all children engaged lifelong readers and learners, the data indicate that schools are failing to meet this worthy goal. The evidence of this failure, in fact, is overwhelming. The National Endowment for the Arts study, *Reading at Risk* (2004), found that fewer young adults read literature now than at any time since World War II. The segment of the population that is least likely to read literature is the group that has just left their formal schooling. The RAND study, *Reading for Understanding: Toward a Research and Development Program in Reading Comprehension* (2002), found in an international study of comprehension that U.S. 11th graders placed near the bottom, behind students from the Philippines, Brazil, Indonesia, and many other developing nations. Our own NAEP 2005 (National Assessment of Educational Progress) found that though younger readers in the U.S. improved their scores, 7th and 11th graders scored lower than previously. The 2003 NAEP found that only 6 percent of American high school seniors were reading at an advanced level, defined in part by the ability to identify main ideas and support their choices with evidence in the text, and the ability to see patterns inside and across texts (these are two seminal tools of inquiry). In the 1992 National Adult Literacy Survey (Kirsch et al., 1993), only 2 percent of young adults (ages 16–24) scored at the highest level of 5, defined as the capacity to ask their own questions, manage their own learning processes, independently choose their own reading, and apply their own knowledge in interactions with the world—all skills that are developed by an inquiry approach.

These assessments show that American students are proficient with such basic literacy skills as literal decoding and formulaic writing but fail to approach anything near an advanced level of literacy. Deb Brandt, in her award-winning book *Literacy in American Lives* (2001), argues that the literacy demands of today's world are far greater than they ever have been before. A high level of literacy is central to academic, economic, and social success. "Rising values of advanced skills, propelled by new literacy-based technologies, deflate the value of basic literacy in the marketplace today." (p. 29).

What Does a Nineteenth-Century Shoe Factory Have to Do With the Global Economy?

Well, the answer should be an emphatic *nothing*, but in fact shoes and schooling are indeed linked to why the United States is losing its edge in the twenty-first-century economy. Take, for example, current school structures such as the 45-minute period and single-subject classes. They're based on Horace Mann's nineteenth-century shoe-factory model. Learning is treated as a kind of piecework instead of being situated in coherent experiences organized around real problems. We learn how to make buckles (or learn about algorithmic progressions) in one class and soles (or rates of decay) in another, but we never learn how to make a whole shoe (or to apply various mathematical understandings to deal with the problems of extinction and survival). Decontextualized, fragmented instruction persists, although we now know learners benefit from extended periods of engagement with integrated curricula applied to real problems in real situations. After all, in real life we do not arbitrarily separate what we know into subjects but learn and apply whatever is needed to solve the problem at hand. Long gone are the days when kids in school might go on to become workers in a shoe factory, yet we still teach them that way.

The Wake-Up Call No One Answered

In the early 1980s, several scholars called for school reform (see Boyer, 1985; Sizer, 1984). Among the most widely read books was John Goodlad's *A Place Called School* (1984), which bemoaned the information-driven, teacher-centered lecture format. What he called for was something similar to the inquiry method. But recently, Goodlad has reported that despite numerous reform initiatives, classroom culture and practices have remained essentially unchanged (2003).

In a series of studies, Nystrand et al. (1996, 1997) found the occurrence of actual classroom dialogue and inquiry/research (as opposed to recitation/coverage) to be incredibly rare. In fact, most of what teachers identified as discussion in their own classrooms, Nystrand found to be recitation (thinly veiled lectures). Disturbingly, this seems to be particularly true in lower-track classes. In fact, a recent Center for English Language and Achievement (CELA) study (Applebee et al., 2003) reported that the researchers could not find enough authentic discussion in lower-track classes to study it! Despite Delpit's (1995) and Lee's (2001) calls for authentic discussion and "dialogic" instruction to become standard for all classes of all students in all schools, particularly for students who have struggled as learners or have been marginalized by society, these classrooms remain stringently monologic (i.e., the only substantive contributions are determined by the teacher and the curriculum). Nobel laureate Carl Wieman's research (2005) shows that information transmission actually undermines scientific understanding and enthusiasm for science. In our studies of boys' literacy, Michael Smith and I (2002, 2006) likewise found that traditional instruction put struggling students into a double bind formed by their deficient skills and boring and degrading instructional practices that failed to engage them or help them.

Why Haven't the Proposed Reforms Been Implemented?

Why is meaningful inquiry and exploratory dialogue so rare in American schools, despite the fact that leading researchers agree that they are essential to student learning? (In addition to those mentioned above, see Applebee, 1996; Hillocks, 1999, 2002; Langer, 2001.)

According to University of Wisconsin researcher Ken Zeichner (see, for example, Zeichner & Tabachnik, 1981), teaching and schools are essentially conservative. They fail to make use of advances in research on learning because of the "salience of the traditional." School structures, parental expectations, and outmoded testing and accountability procedures keep us from making the changes that cognitive science, literacy research, and our own reflective experience show we need to make.

More specifically, we have failed to encourage teachers to put these reforms into practice, and we have failed to teach them how to do it. Teachers may not know how to teach meaningfully and democratically, and they may not have had any help in learning how. Studies of change and development among teachers (e.g., Tharp & Gallimore, 1988) show that they, like students, need assistance and support over time to move through their own zones of proximal development. Assistance and time: that's what it takes to learn new practices, particularly when the learners are already overburdened by other concerns (as most teachers are).

Another reason these reforms have stalled is the pressure for coverage and high-stakes testing. The cheapest and easiest thing to test is information, so that's what standardized tests inevitably test for, even when they purport not to (for example, writing prompts tend to measure whether students possess enough information to respond, instead of actual writing capacity [Hillocks, 2002]).

Despite these challenges, to truly prepare students to be substantive thinkers and democratic citizens, we need to move from the tyranny of information-transmission teaching that dominates American education to inquiry-based teaching. There is no cost to this move, since it actually improves students' performance on standardized tests, as it improves their engagement, understanding, and ability to apply what they have learned.

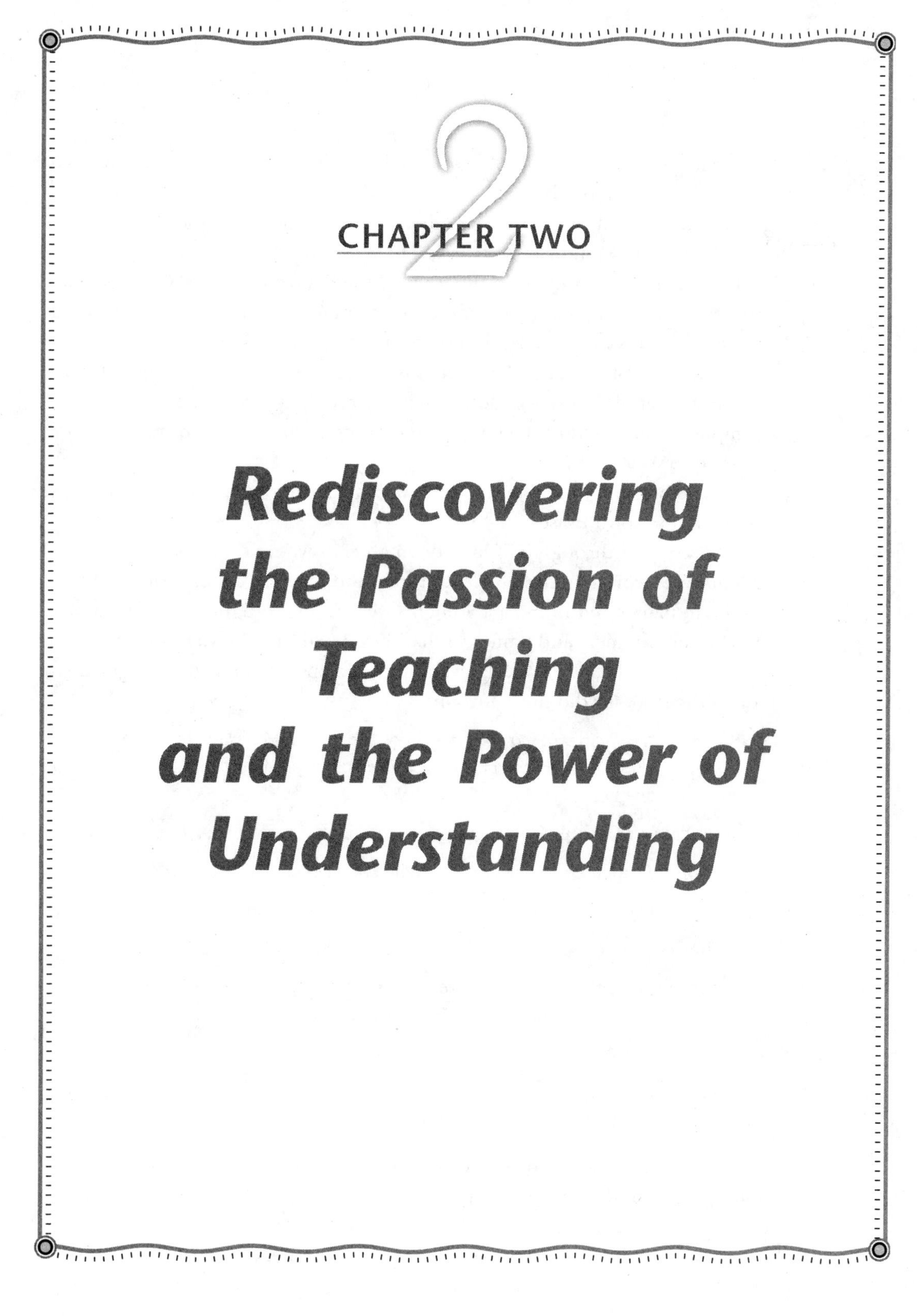

CHAPTER TWO

Rediscovering the Passion of Teaching and the Power of Understanding

Let me give you portraits of two schools, one in which students are at desks hitting the snooze button and one in which wide-awake learning is occurring. This morning in a suburban school near my home, I observed two junior high classes. The teachers both stood at a podium, lecturing their sixth graders on the topic of the day. In one class, the topic was correcting a run-on sentence; in the other, students were covering background information on Native American history. In both, the desks were lined up, facing the front of the class. The students were supposed to be taking notes, but they mostly stared into space. Both teachers were operating under the assumption that teaching is telling, and learning is taking in information purveyed to you.

By late morning, I had entered the Foothills School, an alternative K–9 school in downtown Boise.

I walked first through a fifth-grade math class where small groups of students were working on a puzzle known as the "curious cube." The cube was covered in names and numbers. Students were trying to figure out the patterns between the numbers and names so that they could predict what was on the bottom of the cube. There were several possible answers that could be justified, though the students did not know this.

Joe: It's a girl's name on one side of the cube and always boys' names on the others. Since Frank is on the top, there has to be a girl's name on the bottom.

Amanda: Is that right? (Turning the cube) Rob—Roberta . . . Alfred—Alma.

Tom: What about the numbers? What do the lower ones mean?

Joe: I think they mean the number of syllables in the name.

Tracy: That works for Alfred and Alma but not for Rob and Roberta.

Teacher: Remember that your theory has to explain all the elements in the pattern, and how they are connected.

Joe: Darn it all!

Amanda: I wonder if the numbers on opposite sides add up to something, or if what they add up to forms a pattern.

The students quickly began to add the numbers and then proceeded to multiply them and perform other operations. Once they solve the puzzle, they will make their own cube puzzles that display various semantic and mathematical relationships between words and numbers.

After I left the math classroom, I wandered through the third- and fourth-grade open space. The students were in small groups, at stations scattered around the classroom, where they had built Lego cars. Chris, the teacher, was posing a problem to the students: "Your challenge is to power your car using energy that is stored in the rubber band. How do you think you can store that energy?"

One boy jumped up and said, "Twist it; let it go!"

A girl said, "You could stretch it and let it go too!"

A second boy argued, "But you can't use the energy unless you connect it somehow to the axle or wheels on the car. You have to, like, transfer it—the energy, I mean—to the car."

Chris asked, "How many tries do you think it will take to do that?"

A chorus of guesses, mostly big numbers, were yelled out.

"So what will you do if you get frustrated?" Chris asked.

"Rip up paper!"

"Be flexible. Just keep trying stuff."

"Learn from your mistakes. You will keep getting closer!"

"Ask for help."

"Work with your team! Learn from others and share ideas!"

"Take a deep breath."

"Walk around and think about it!"

"These are excellent ideas," Chris said. "Get to work and if you get frustrated use one of those strategies. Remember to keep track of what works best and what doesn't work so you can report it to others. Learning means you have to make some mistakes and hit some dead ends, so that is good stuff, too!"

From Chris's class I went to the sixth-grade room. The students were talking about forms of prejudice evident in the school and what they could do about them. The discussion was intense.

Jazz: We're supposed to be, like, this alternative school and all about exploration, but people get made fun of for what they wear or if they are interested in different kinds of things.

Julia: What do you mean? Who gets made fun of?

Jazz: Like if you wear sweat clothes. It's like it's not okay to be a jock. It's like there is prejudice against being an athlete or something.

Charlie: I think it's the jocks who are prejudiced. I think it's like people group up and then they make fun of other groups. It's like prejudice is a kind of competition, like we're better than you and that makes you worse.

Joe: Like you're not as worthy.

Teacher: So, what is the cause of prejudice? I've heard several things. (Writes on the board.) *Insecurity? Trying to be better by putting others down? Being in a group and wanting to show you are unique?*

Jazz: That's the big problem. That's the really big problem.

Teacher: And what can you do when you feel your rights are threatened or you're suffering prejudice?

Julia: I think the first problem is recognizing what prejudice is, and the cause . . .

Jazz: You'd have to get people to notice their own prejudice—that is really hard to do.

Teacher: What do you think can help people to see their own biases?

The students were then asked to write journal entries theorizing about the causes of prejudice and how people might overcome their own prejudice.

The two junior-high classes at the first school were taught in the information-transmission style, and when those poor sixth graders headed home, they probably would have learned close to nil. There would be no intense conversations ringing in their minds, no memories of emotional or intellectual engagement. But think about what the students in the Foothills school walked away with: memories of *participating* in lessons organized around real-world problems (how to see and interpret patterns, how to transfer energy, how to work together, how to deal with frustration, how to identify and overcome prejudice) and how to solve these problems.

Both their conceptual knowledge and their procedural knowledge were developed and used as tools in the context of solving a problem, with much the same immediacy as a carpenter using a plane to smooth an edge of wood. This "toolishness" is essential: information and facts must become concepts and strategies that have heuristic value. *Heuristic*, which comes from the same Greek root as the word *eureka*, simply means that what has been learned has become part of a problem-solving repertoire and can be used to do something. In these ways, the Foothills examples demonstrate inquiry approaches (Smith & Wilhelm, 2002, 2006): they exemplify how disciplines work by asking students big questions and helping them use ideas and processes as tools to get a job done. The job might be as tangible as applying a geometric principle to home building, or it might be more abstract, perhaps advancing one's understanding of a moral issue. Inquiry inducts students into a community of practice; they come to think and act more like people who work with the disciplines of math, science, social science, ethics, literature, philosophy, government.

Transformative Teaching: 5 First Actions to Take

So what do we do once we've moved the desks out of the neat perennial rows, moved away from lecture and recitation, and moved our minds toward an inquiry approach? In this section, we'll look at some of the first things you can do "tomorrow" to evolve your teaching. Later in the chapter, on page 30, I invite you to try an activity that will help you examine your beliefs about teaching and learning.

1. Teach So It Matters

First, think about how to reconceptualize your role and that of your students as members of an inquiring community that shares a common vocabulary and a set of conceptual tools and strategic practices to solve open problems in a discipline. To discover problems worth pursuing, think about what matters to you, and what matters to your students, and jot it down on a piece of paper. Then make connections—literally and figuratively—between these passions and concerns and the content of your curriculum (see Chapter 3). These are the first sketches of your design for an inquiring community.

Take This Quick Quiz!

Think of the most recent text you have read.

- Why did you read this text? Did you choose it freely or was it assigned?
- What did you already know about the topic of the text?
- Did you already have an interest in the topic?
- Were you able to use what you learned by thinking with it, arguing with it, talking about it, or applying it in some way?

When I give this quiz to middle schoolers, more than 85 percent reply that the last thing they read was an assigned text, that they knew very little about the topic, had no interest in it, and saw little use for what they "learned" from it.

In contrast, when I survey adults and nearly 90 percent say they read something they freely chose, nearly 100 percent say that it was of interest to them, they already knew something about the topic, and they saw an immediate use for the information. Those few adults who were assigned texts to read were part of a book club or a graduate course in which they were willing participants. Their reading provided them with clear, immediate satisfactions and they were able to use it to accomplish a task or think about their lives.

If we want to make the reading, writing, and learning kids do in school more like the reading, writing, and learning adults do in the world, we need to connect assignments to what matters to students. We need to show them how the material relates to their lives and their needs, and we need to provide them with opportunities to engage with and use what they learn.

2. Review and Renew Your Memberships

As adults, we participate in many different communities of practice, made up of people who share our interests in disciplinary work (Lave & Wenger, 1991), as well as those who share our passions for avocations and hobbies, such as bird-watching, knitting, basketball, book reading, carpentry (Gee, 2003). Disciplinary and affinity groups are organized to develop and enact particular kinds of work, and they develop language, concepts, and strategies to do this work.

The process of becoming a member of a sustained community of practice *is* learning. And as Lave and Wenger point out, learning has two intertwined aspects—emerging identity and emerging expertise: "Developing an identity as a member of a community and becoming knowledgeably skillful are part of the same process" (p. 65). Think about your own professional and personal connections and how these define and enrich your identity. You and your colleagues have a particular lingo (discourse) for doing the work of planning instruction, for interacting with one another and with students and parents, and for evaluating student progress. We talk about "IEPs" and "AYP," about objectives and benchmarks, portfolios and performance standards. Knowing the discourse and the practices of the community displays your competence and identity as a member, as someone who can talk the talk and walk the walk. If you play golf, belong to a music group, or coach kids' sports, you also possess the language and skills and are versed in the rituals of these groups. Waiters, librarians, kayakers, video gamers, civil engineers, musicians, and all other people engaged with a group that uses specialized language and sets of practices belong to a community of practice. So do punk rockers, feminists, conservatives, liberals, and basketball fans. And kids have these communities of practice, too. Think about all the interests they share with others—video games, sports, arts, playing music, reading anime, and many more.

With inquiry, we help students become

Teaching How to *Inquire*

To induct students into a new community of practice, we must teach them both how to inquire and how to take on the identity of a particular kind of inquirer. This requires them to learn new discourses (the ability to use new concepts, vocabulary, and ways of performing the group's work and communicating with one another about this work) and ways of thinking with these discourses that mirror those in the community of experts. To do so, according to Resnick (1999), teachers need to do the following:

- model and assist students in using accurate and relevant discipline-based talk
- promote and model discipline-based thinking and learning
- join knowledge and thinking with learning new disciplinary understandings
- collaborate with students in joint problem solving of the kind used in the community of practice
- engage in appropriate critical inquiry and knowledge production, which is the work of a community of practice

aware of—and become adept at—working with an array of communities, which is synonymous with learning how to think and act like experts. We can only do this by using the identities and the knowledge they have as a bridge to the new identity and knowledge to be learned. To quote James Gee (2003, p. 51): "All learning in all semiotic domains requires identity work. It requires taking on a new identity and forming bridges from one's old identities to the new one. For example, a child in a science classroom engaged in real inquiry, and not passive learning, must be willing to take on an identity as a certain type of scientific thinker, problem-solver and doer. The child must see and make connections between this new identity and other identities he or she has already formed." Gee strongly asserts the importance of promoting students' new identities, and growing their new competence by building on their existing competence: "If children cannot or will not make bridges between one or more of their real-world identities and the virtual identity at stake in the classroom (e.g., being a particular type of scientist)—or if teachers or others destroy or don't help build such bridges, then learning is imperiled" (p. 61).

"Being told is the opposite of finding out."
—Jimmy Britton

3. Shift Your Stance to Show-How

To build students' know-how, we have to model, mentor, and monitor student performance. When we tell—only imparting information to our students—they tend to forget much of it within two weeks and practically all of it within two years (Tyler, 1949). But research in situated cognition (Brown et al., 1989) has found that when we teach students *how* in a meaningful context, students have the

Three Conditions for Understanding

Briane Cambourne (2002) lists these among the core assumptions of the learning-centered inquiry model (or socio-constructivist model):

1. Learning occurs in a context and cannot be separated from or achieved apart from a meaningful context in which it is developed and applied.
2. The learner's background, current understandings, immediate purposes, and goals are central to what is learned.
3. Knowledge is constructed socially through interaction that includes questioning, negotiation, dialogue, evaluation, and ultimately, transformation of understanding and the transformation of the learner from that of a more novice practitioner to a more expert one. The goal of learning is not information but "knowledge," which requires deep understanding and application.

(For a discussion of the important differences between information and knowledge, see Wilhelm, 2003.)

motivation to use the conceptual material. Through doing, they learn more deeply, and retain what they learn.

For example, when I wanted to learn to kayak, I read several books and watched kayakers on the river near my home. But I did this knowing that I would soon be kayaking on the river, and that my real learning would begin when I got on the river. The water immediately communicated to me when I had done something wrong (because I would be upside down!) and when things had gone well (because I would have successfully navigated a set of drops or rapids or would be surfing joyously on the foam pillow behind a "hole"). With the help of other kayakers, I could make adaptations to my technique and would immediately see what happened as a result.

Think about your own teaching. Sure, you can benefit from reading books about teaching and from taking methods courses, but you really learn how to teach from your students, when you try to implement your instructional ideas. The process of purposefully teaching (why and how) content (what) to students (who) in the situation of the classroom (when and where) is what really develops your expertise.

4. Recast Yourself as a Co-Collaborator

An inquiry approach blows the adage "Those who can't do, teach" out of the water because it requires you to dive in to the big questions and "do" the discipline along with your students. There's no room for "can't"! Society may have been able to slap that destructive label on teachers locked in to the information-transmission model, but it won't stick to those who embrace the spirit of inquiry and cognitive research.

The teacher who apprentices students into doing the discipline must not only know how to read, write, learn, and converse as an expert, but must know *how* to assist and support students to do the same. Those who teach, *must do*!

Going the Way of the Model T?

Are these models for teaching and learning outdated?

The topical coverage model—also known as the curriculum-centered or teacher-centered approach—is now called into question by many cognitive researchers (see, e.g., Rogoff, Matusov, & White, 1996), who fault it for being too focused on the *what*. In this model, teachers generally lecture and assign readings; students memorize information and take informational tests.

The student-centered model—also known as natural learning and discovery methods—is also critiqued by these researchers. The concern is that the model focuses too exclusively on the *who*—namely, the learner and her current interests, desires, goals, and idiosyncratic, personal (vs. disciplinary) understandings.

5. Teach for Understanding

Recent cognitive research promotes a multisided model that highlights the collaborative interactions and relationships between the teacher and the students, between the students and the content, and among the students and content and real-world situations. This focus allows us to teach for deep, disciplinary understanding and includes a consideration of:

- the what (the content to be learned)
- the multiple whos (I may sound like Dr. Seuss, but I mean here the teacher and all of the learners, their prior knowledge and abilities, and the community of practice.)
- the how (the expert procedures and strategies we must know to operate on and use the content, and to understand how knowledge is developed and deployed by experts)
- the why, where, and when (the purpose, situational contexts, and uses of the knowledge that is being constructed through the various learning interactions) (For more detailed accounts of the student-centered model, the topical coverage model and the multisided model, see Wilhelm, Baker & Dube-Hackett, 2001; and also Wilhelm, 2001, 2002, 2004.)

One more very important point: The learning-centered, inquiry approach is the *only* model that promotes democracy. The information-transmission approach is authoritarian in how it defines what must be learned and thought. The student-centered is individualistic. Only inquiry promotes learning together about how to participate usefully in a community. Only inquiry apprentices students to independence in thought, judgment, and problem-solving processes according to community and disciplinary norms.

Which Metaphor Do You Buy?

Information-transmission: Start your engines and drive the curricular race course! Teaching is autocratic, sitting in the driver's seat and zooming through information. Learning is "fueling up" with information from a backseat perch and doing the laps of a prescribed loop. (Note: the word *curriculum* comes from the Latin word for "race course.")

Student-centered: Make your own path! You must be your own teacher. Teaching is about nurturing and stepping aside. Learning is self-discovery. No roadmap required.

Inquiry/learning-centered: A wondrous road trip in which teachers and students take a collaborative journey toward disciplinary understanding. Exact destination unknown, but road maps and resources are valued, and specific navigation strategies are learned along the way. Teaching is authoritative (not authoritarian), participatory, collaborative. The teacher acts as a mentor and guide.

Only inquiry requires that students respectfully collaborate with one another.

If you can reflect on these five actions and make them your own, you'll be on your way! In the next section, I invite you to discover how "natural" our preference for inquiry-rich discourse is—regardless of whether we are "doing" enough of it as teachers.

What Is the Best Classroom Discourse?

Let's turn now to a consideration of what you believe to be the role of questioning and classroom conversation in promoting learning. We'll use this activity as an entry point for discussion of how to promote inquiry-driven discourse at both the unit and the lesson levels.

Over the past ten years, I have tracked the responses of more than three thousand teachers to this ranking activity. (It was first created by my friend Michael Smith.) I will share those results with you after you complete your own ranking.

Directions

Read through the four short transcripts, assuming that they are representative excerpts of much longer discussions. For ease of comparison, assume that these discussions all took place in seventh-grade classrooms of average ability.

Rank them from the best example of class discussion (1) to the worst (4). Be prepared to explain your reasoning, which will express a theoretical position on teaching and learning.

Some readers have difficulty following transcript B, so let me explain that the group in this transcript is trying to discover the final digit of 7 to the fifth power by extrapolating patterns without actually doing the multiplication. (It's helpful to know that $7^0 = 1$; $7^1 = 7$; $7^2 = 49$; $7^3 = 343$, $7^4 = 2{,}401$, and $7^5 = 16{,}807$. Students are trying to discern and extrapolate the sequence of final digits, which goes 1, 7, 9, 3, 1, 7, 9, 3, 1, ...)

The other three transcripts are fairly self-explanatory and come from social studies, English, and science classrooms.

To help you develop your criteria for ranking the teaching demonstrated in the transcripts, consider the following questions:

1 What are the standards for good classroom discussions?

2. What are the most powerful purposes and outcomes of good classroom discussion?
3. What are the qualities that mark good classroom discussions?
4. What should be the students' role and the teacher's role in a good classroom discussion?
5. What moves should a teacher make to facilitate good classroom discussion? What moves should the students be making?
6. What does a good discussion look, sound, and feel like to participants? To observers?

(Note: I will address these questions in depth later in this chapter and throughout the rest of the book.)

A. RANK: ________________

Context: From a historical discussion introducing *To Kill a Mockingbird.*

Source: Marty Nystrand, University of Wisconsin–Madison

Teacher: All right. How did the South, how did most people in the South earn their living before the Civil War? Roger?

Student 1: Huge farms.

Teacher: Okay, huge, huge farms, plantations, right? All that farming takes lots and lots of laborers. If you had laborers that you didn't have to pay, you sure as heck were gonna get a better deal in life—much more profit than if you had to pay people to come and pick your cotton for you. Okay? So what do you suppose happened to all these farms, after the Civil War, after all these people had to either pay their slaves or set them free? What happened to the farms?

Student 2: They stopped.

Teacher: That's right. They were toast. They're done. All right? Only the people who had lots and lots of money could manage to keep these huge, huge plantations going. So the South, as a result of the Civil War, was economically ruined, wiped out. Their major source of income, the plantation system, and farming, that was done for. All right? So naturally many of these farmers are gonna be bitter. They're gonna be upset. And how do you suppose they're gonna treat the black people who used to be slaves? Jane, you want to comment on that?

Student 3: Well, like, didn't some of the blacks stay on the plantations when the war ended?

Teacher: Um-hmm. Some of them did. But it was illegal for them to be kept (that is, enslaved) there. . . . How do you suppose the people felt toward the blacks? Come on, they lost their source of income! What's gonna be their attitude?

Student 3: They resented them.

Teacher: Sure! They resented them. They placed the blame on them—pay attention. All right? They blamed them. So how're they gonna treat 'em?

Student 4: Terribly.

B. RANK: ________________

Context: Discussion of the final digit of 7^5.

Source: Lampert, Magdalene. (1990).

Teacher: Arthur, why do you think it's 1?

Student 1: Because 7^4 ends in 1, then it's times 1 again.

Student 2: The answer to 7^4 is 2,401. You multiply that by 7 to get the answer, so it's 7 times 1.

Teacher: Why 9, Sarah?

Student 3: I think Sarah thought the number should be 49.

Student 2: Maybe they think it goes 9, 1, 9, 1, 9, 1.

Student 4: I know it's 7, cause 7—

Student 5: Because 7^4 ends in 1, so if you times it by 7, it'll end in 7.

Student 6: I think it's 7. No, I think it's 8.

Student 7: I don't think it's 8 because, it's odd number times odd number, and that's always an odd number.

Student 8: It's 7 because it's like saying 49 times 49 times 7.

Student 1: I still think it's 1, because you do 7 times 7 to get 49 and then for 7^4 you do 49 times 49 and for 7^5 times itself and that will end in 1.

Teacher: What's 49?

Student 9: 2,401.

Teacher: Arthur's theory is that 7^5 should be 2,401 times 2,401 and since there's a 1 here and a 1 here—

Student 9: It's 2,401 times 7.

Student 2: I have a proof that it won't be a 9. It can't be 9, 1, 9, 1, because 7^3 ends in a 3.

Student 6: I think it goes 1, 7, 9, 1, 7, 9, 1, 7, 9.

Teacher: What about 7^3 ending in 3? The last number ends in . . . 9 times 7 is 63.

Student 6: Oh . . .

Student 8: Abdul's thing isn't wrong, 'cause it works. He said times the last digit by 7 and the last digit is 9, so the last one will be 3. It's 1, 7, 9, 3, 1, 7, 9, 3.

Student 1: I want to revise my thinking. It would be 7 times 7 times 7 times 7 times 7. I was thinking it would be 7 times 7 times 7 times 7 times 7 times 7 times 7 times 7.

C. RANK: ________________

Context: Student has just read his plot summary of a chapter of *Roll of Thunder, Hear My Cry*.

Source: Nystrand, Marty, & Gamoran, Adam (1991).

Teacher: (*To the class as a whole, referring to John's plot summary*) Wow! What do you think about that?

Student 1: It was very thorough.

Teacher: Yeah, pretty thorough. I had a lot of trouble getting everything down (*writes on the board*), and I think I missed the part about trying to boycott. (*Reads from the board*) "And tries to organize a boycott." Did I get everything down, John, that you said?

Student 1: What about the guy who didn't really think these kids were a pest?

Teacher: Yeah, okay. What's his name? Do you remember?

Student 1: (*Indicates that he can't remember.*)

Student 2: Wasn't it Turner?

Teacher: Was it Turner?

Students: Yes.

Teacher: Okay, so Mr. Turner resisted help. Why? Why would he want to keep shopping at that terrible store?

Student 1: There was only one store to buy from because all the other ones were white.

Teacher: Well, the Wallace store was white, too.

Student 3: (*Addressing Student 1*) Is it Mr. Hollings' store? Is that it?

Student 1: No. Here's the reason. They don't get paid till the cotton comes in. But throughout the year they still have to buy stuff—food, clothes, seed, and stuff like that. So the owner of the plantation will sign for what they buy at the store so that throughout the year they can still buy stuff on credit.

Teacher: (*Writing on board*) So "he has to have credit in order to buy things, and this store is the only one that will give it to him."

(*Student 1 continues with explanation, as Teacher writes it on the chalkboard.*)

Student 4: I was just going to say, "It was the closest store."

Teacher: (*Writing on chalkboard*) Okay—it's the closest store; it seems to be in the middle of the area; a lot of sharecroppers who don't get paid cash—they get credit at the store—and its very hard to get credit at other stores. So it's going to be very hard for her to organize that boycott; she needs to exist on credit. Yeah? (*Nods to another student*)

D. RANK: ________________

Context: Review of a lesson on magnetism.

Source: Bulman, Lesley. (1985).

Teacher: Earth spins about an axis. The point at the top around which it spins is called what? What's it called?

Student 1: The geographical axis.

Teacher: Geographical . . . ? The point at the top. Almost right. Yes, David?

Student 2: North.

Teacher: Yes, north. And the point at which the magnet appears to be—at the top there, just underneath the ground—what's the name of that point there?

Student 3: Magnetic north.

Teacher: Magnetic north. If I was standing on the top of the magnetic north with a compass, what would it do?

Student 4: It would go round and round and round.

Teacher: It wouldn't point in any direction at all. Supposing if I was standing at the geographic north, what would it do there?

Student 5: Point to the magnetic north.

Teacher: Right. What was the name of this angle between the magnetic and the geographical north? Yes, Gary?

Student 6: Angle of declination.

Teacher: Angle of declination. Right, there's a difficult one. Now, I've put a spot there—that's supposed to represent the magnetic north—and the geographic north is the point at which it spins around. Now, if I come down that line there to a point there, can anyone tell me what the angle of declination is going to be? Yes, Bill?

Student 7: Nought.

Teacher: Nought. Yes. There's no angle between the magnetic north and the geographical north. They're both on the same line.

Ranking the Discussions

During the ten years I have administered this ranking, I have had fewer than 40 out of more than 3,000 teachers choose A or D as the best example of classroom discourse, just a bit over 1 percent. After the teachers have small-group discussions to reach consensus on rankings, *all* teachers choose B or C as the best example. Almost 60 percent choose B as the best example, and slightly more than 40 percent choose C. Many who choose C admit to being confused by the math in B.

Research shows that actual classroom discussion rarely if ever approaches what we see in B and C. When explaining their reasons for choosing B or C, teachers summarize the most important findings of the research on effective classroom questioning and discussion, as well as research on inquiry models of teaching. This means that most teachers have an intuitive, if not explicit, understanding of the inquiry method. *Yet this kind of teaching rarely takes place in schools!* (See Nystrand, 1997.)

What Gives?

Teachers can identify effective teaching, and even intuit the principles behind it, but they don't incorporate these principles in their own classrooms. I have some theories about why this is. First, I'll review what the teachers say about the transcripts, and I'll map their responses to current sociocultural theory and research. Then, I'll take a stab at why teachers put so little of what they believe into practice. We will consider how to overcome these obstacles. The remainder of the book is dedicated to practical teaching strategies for implementing the kind of inquiry supported by cognitive research *and* the teacher responses to this ranking.

What Teachers Said

What beliefs and thoughts led the teachers to give transcripts B and C the highest ranks? Here, I've summarized the teachers' comments. In italics I've added my own two cents to amplify the teacher's insights.

- The B and C discussions are alike in their problem- or task-orientation. For example, in B—"How many ways are there to find out the final digit of 7 to the fifth power?"—the task is to explore and evaluate various possibilities for solving a particular problem. In C—"What is the best possible summary of this section of the book?"—the task is to create a succinct synthesis of ideas. *The richness of this summary is that it's not an isolated exercise or an end in itself—summarizing will help these students with subsequent reading and interpretation.*
- The task in B invites students to create new understandings and define applications. As such, it's a form of critical inquiry. In the midst of discussion, students use math concepts and strategies as tools to complete the task. *Yes! They are novice experts interacting as a community of practice. Their work and discourse approximates the ways mathematicians discuss and practice math. The correspondence concept is being approached.*
- The task in C invites students to inquire in order to organize, understand, or use established sets of information. As such, it's topical research. *Both B and C are examples of inquiry, but B, as critical inquiry, is more sophisticated and advanced (more on this in a bit).*

Following is a list of attributes of good discussion that teachers have identified through this activity.

Effective Discussions: The Teachers' List of Attributes

Inquiry-oriented discussions:

- build off of a big, initial question that provides a clear purpose; the big question declares the problem or a task to be tackled.
- generate new, compelling open-ended questions that are posed and pursued by both teachers and students.
- invite exploration; participants play around and take risks as they pursue answers to the big idea (engage in "bricolage").
- encourage students to feel free to put forth tentative theories (using language like *maybe, perhaps, theory*).

- allow students to do the work, and do it together. Many students talk.
- focus on compelling ideas and significant processes—not just on getting a single correct answer. (In fact, the correct answer is cited twice near the beginning of example B and conversation continues.)
- entertain various perspectives and cultivate students' appreciation of—and ability to handle—complexity.
- support the discovery of definable patterns. The conversation centers on *patterns* of details with the implicit notion that these patterns will yield understandings that students can apply in some fashion.
- involve applications that have a place in the real world—applications that don't seem the stuff of school but the stuff of today's culture (whether that be local culture, American society, or the culture of communities of practice).
- encourage students to "take up" one another's ideas. The teacher models how to build on others' ideas or challenge them respectfully. Students talk to one another.
- cast the teacher in the role of a facilitator and guide—not the answer giver.
- invite the teacher to offer timely challenges to clear up misconceptions and ask for clarifications, reasoning, evidence. The teacher provides input *at the point of need* to help students refine theories and pursue the strongest ones.
- are often "mapped" by the teacher, who may write major ideas on a chalkboard or visually map the developing ideas onto a graphic organizer of some kind. These serve to placehold and summarize so that participants see their talk continues to head in a purposeful direction.
- provide the time participants need in order to wrestle with difficult ideas.

Guess what? Even though many of these teachers were not steeped in the research literature on inquiry- and discussion-based learning, the features they identified are articulated in much the same way by foremost researchers in literacy (Applebee, 1996; Hillocks, 1995, 1999, 2002; Langer, 1993, 2001; Nystrand, et al., 1997).

What Teachers Critique

As they did with naming the positive attributes listed above, the teachers were just about unanimous in finding the negative attributes in transcripts A and D. In these discussion transcripts, the teachers seemed locked into simple topical coverage, typified by the teacher:

- dominating the discussion
- ignoring many student responses as irrelevant—the "discussion" has been predetermined, and the teacher already knows what he or she is going to say
- offering few student opportunities to participate
- encouraging only short and informational student responses, not substantive ones that would drive the direction of the talk
- masquerading a lecture as a conversation, with student responses merely filling in the blanks
- requiring students to guess what the teacher already knows rather than creating new understandings together

In sum, the teachers criticize what Nystrand (1997) calls the "recitation" or "monologic" format in A and D. The take-way? Engagement and understanding are supported by dialogue (meaning-making discussion/conversation); they are undermined by monologue (rote recitation).

Next Practical Steps: Three Key Moves

This is the thing: We can *always* reframe information-driven teaching into inquiry. Anything we already do in school can be done in ways that will lead to more powerful and transferable learning. In the next chapter, I will describe how to do this reframing, and how it can be done both through your daily activities and interactions with students and on a more extended unit level.

There are three basic steps for creating an inquiry-oriented classroom:

1. **Identify an essential question and associated enduring understandings:** I begin by reframing the curricular topic into a guiding question pursued by the discipline. Then I identify enduring disciplinary

understandings and processes necessary to addressing the question, the ones used by experts in the field. This means figuring out the heart of the matter—why this knowledge was developed in the first place and why it is taught and used in the world beyond school.

2. **Identify a final project:** Next, I identify projects that kids can do at the end of the unit that will demonstrate their understanding—their mastery and use of the enduring concepts and tools for dealing with the essential question. You have to know where you want your students to go, and how you will know they have arrived. At the end of your instructional sequence, what will your students know and do and how can they demonstrate this mastery? Consider such options as writing, dramas, museum exhibits, video documentaries, Web sites, and social-action projects.

3. **Create a "backwards plan":** This is the most important step and the hardest to enact. The backwards plan (or instructional sequence) is a carefully ordered set of activities that support students' progress—text by text and activity by activity—toward their ability to complete the final project independently. This is the instruction that moves students from their current capacities through their zones of proximal development (what is possible for them to achieve with assistance), to the point where they have developed the expert tools they will use in their final projects. An important part of this plan, and the focus of this book, is the creation of classroom activities, conversations, questioning schemes, and student-generated questions that help students know and do more than they currently can, and help them think and talk more like disciplinary experts. The backwards plan is about putting each day's activities in service of the goal of students' achieving deep understanding and being able to engage in "meaningful making" that uses the concepts and strategies they have learned to do the disciplinary work, i.e., to move students to the correspondence concept. (See Smith and Wilhelm, 2006.)

"Every lesson, activity, or unit must lead to visible and significant change in student thinking, understanding, and behavior, or learning has not occurred."

One Final Quiz

I'm going to give you one last self-reflection quiz before we move on to the next chapter.

In my work with preservice and in-service teachers, I challenge them to think about what kids will say about their class when they are picked up after school, and what if anything they will remember and talk about years down the road. Think about it: We've all had at least one teacher whose positive effects we still feel, even decades later. The teacher we'd like to run into on a hometown visit, or e-mail to thank—though that doesn't seem a strong enough word. We're in awe. We want to say, *Look at who I am! It's partly because of you.* They may have "saved" us, set us up for what we are doing and who we are today. It's big stuff. I want you to be that kind of teacher. I want this book to help you be that teacher. So ask yourself:

- What kind of teacher do I want to be? Which beliefs about students and theories of learning will help me best become that teacher?
- What quality of experience do I want my students to have in my classroom today?
- How will that experience motivate my students for further learning? How do I want their experience to affect their attitudes toward my subject, learning, school, and their futures?
- How will what I do today help my students internalize concepts and tools for immediate use *today* as well as for future learning?
- What will my students say about today's class to their friends at lunch, and to their parents at dinner? Will their words and feelings match my purposes? Will the quality of my teaching and way of interacting with the ideas and issues of the world stay with my students?
- How will today's learning change my students' ways of thinking, acting, and being?

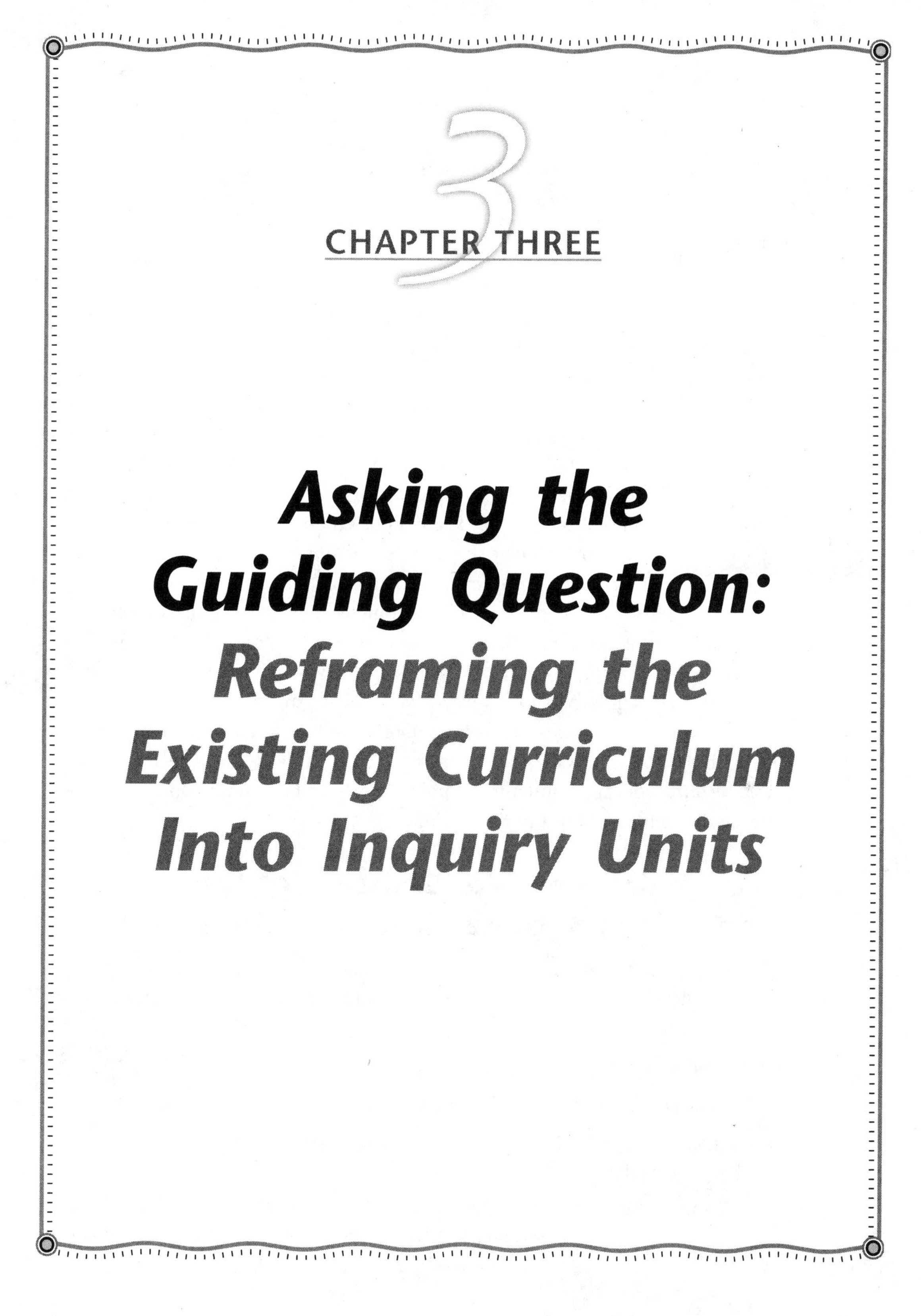

CHAPTER THREE

Asking the Guiding Question: Reframing the Existing Curriculum Into Inquiry Units

I used to do a lot of poor and lifeless teaching. Not that every class now runs like a Cuisinart, but I can honestly say that all of my classes are turbocharged. The kids seem to emit waves of intellectual energy the moment they enter the classroom. I can hardly remember the times when I struggled to interest a class of bored, sleepy faces. What's behind this amazing transformation? I use guiding questions to frame what we do as inquiry. I teach what I have to teach *in a way that matters to kids.* That leads to powerful student questions and animated learning conversations that build understanding.

Think about focusing a camera, twisting the lens back and forth until a panoramic blur becomes crystalline. What a difference! Reframing your existing curriculum brings a similar clarity to content and themes. An interesting challenge—How can we best deal with human cruelty?—becomes a focal point around which all else is oriented. Problem orientation makes learning personally relevant and socially significant. The guiding question reaches into students' lives, arcing from, say, examining a world war to a horrible hazing tragedy at a nearby college. Teaching becomes easier because you now have a compelling hook. Learning becomes as exciting as reading a detective novel. On the way to solving the case, the problem, the vexing question, dialogues occur that consolidate major concepts, vocabulary, strategies, and ideas. The curricular material comes alive—it is current, and it has currency. Everything from the morning newspaper to worn-out textbooks and Web sites has its place as a resource, because students see how the material is relevant—and is used—in the disciplines and out in the world.

Eighth Graders Take On Issues of the Oval Office (and Become Citizens of the World)

Today three girls blow into my classroom like a summer shower, arguing animatedly with one another about the essential question that frames our Holocaust unit: What can we do about evil?

Amanda: I'm just saying that I don't think evil is *natural*!

Sasha: But what difference does that make to what you're arguing?

Amanda: All I'm saying is that I don't think people are born as terrorists. So going out to find and kill them isn't good enough.

Tammy: But what are we going to do about terrorists *right now*? I mean, they are already evil, aren't they? It doesn't mean they were born that way,

but they are not going to change now. And more evil would be done if we didn't go after them!

Amanda: I'm just saying that if evil isn't natural then it gets caused somehow. So we have to try to do something about the causes. We can't just attack what we see . . . the symptoms or whatever. It's like the 9/11 Commission thingy we read. . . .

They keep talking over one another as the other kids breeze into the room. Though this is no rarity, I still can't help thinking: *These are eighth graders. And they are totally engaged.* They see the curricular topic of national security as a problem to be solved. They are relating the Holocaust to the current realities of their lives and the world. I am helping them learn what the curriculum and state learning standards require, but we are doing it with more efficiency, connectivity, and verve. My students are learning how to read, write, argue, and think about how they want to live and be.

Just Follow the Yellow Brick Road: Planning Steps

As I explained at the end of Chapter 2, implementing the inquiry model is a three-step process:

1. Identify an essential question and associated enduring understandings. This identifies and focuses attention on your framing purpose and your major concepts and strategies.
2. Identify a final project. Successful completion should demonstrate student ownership and use of these concepts and strategies.
3. Create a backwards plan. This plan should map out classroom activities, conversations, questioning schemes, and student-generated questions that help students develop and use both conceptual and procedural understanding necessary to conducting the inquiry.

My friend Jeff Golub once shared with me his "world's most efficient unit-planning guide," which describes the process in similar terms:

1. What is our focus and why does it matter? (essential question and enduring understandings)

2 Where do we want to go with it? (culminating project)

3 Why do we want to go there? (purpose—personally relevant and significant to the discipline)

4 How can students be helped to get there? (backwards plan: instructional sequence that develops the requisite knowledge and skills)

5 How will we know we have arrived? (critical standards for culminating project; assessment)

Step One: Compose Your Own Guiding Questions

In our work at the inquiry-oriented adolescent literacy national demonstration sites in Maine and Utah, my colleagues and I make use of the work of several researchers on asking essential questions (Jacobs, 1989; Travers, 1998; Wiggins & McTighe, 1998, 2003). We have distilled their ideas down to the following criteria.

Essential Question Criteria

An essential question:

- honors students' "reality principle." It addresses their point of view and need for an inquiry to be interesting and relevant in *their* terms.
- addresses the "heart of the discipline" being studied. Essential disciplinary knowledge will be required to answer it.
- possesses emotive force, intellectual bite, or edginess. It invites students into ongoing conversations and debates about real-world disciplinary issues.
- is open-ended, possible to contend, arguable. It must be complex enough to house multiple perspectives and possible answers.
- is concise and clearly stated.
- is linked to data. There are available resources to use in the pursuit of answers.
- may lead to new questions asked by the students. (This is how topical research is extended into critical inquiries.)

How to Reframe the Standards Into Essential Questions

Most curricular topics are worthy of study. Why? Because back in the day, each of them began as inquiry. The "knowledge sets" in any unit, in any discipline, were created or discovered in response to a real-world problem or pressing question. For example, calculus was invented to study moving bodies and make predictions about them. The study of history developed in ancient times as a way to preserve particular cultures, to learn from the past, establish effective governments, and win wars. Economics has evolved to help societies set policies that will produce wealth. Ecology arose to address problems caused by industrial society's impact on the planet's ecological balance.

Most curriculum standards are sensible, even when they aren't ideally articulated. They help us decide what's necessary for students to learn and give us a way to assess our curricula. Besides, standards were never meant to be etched in stone. As a member of the NCTE/IRA SPELA (standards project for English/language arts) team, I know that standards were written to be living documents, a basis for professional discussion that should be continuously revised. The important thing to remember is that any curricular standard can be reframed into an essential question. A good standards-based guiding question will address many other standards and curricular topics and bring them together as a coherent, integrated whole. And coherence is essential when it comes to standards, particularly in language arts. The standards tend to be process- or product-oriented and, as such, are oddly devoid of content or a wider context of ideas. For example, here are some of Rhode Island's high school language arts standards:

- Student produces a response to literature and supports a judgment with evidence from the text.
- Student produces a persuasive essay.
- Student prepares and delivers an individual presentation.

These strike me more as goals than standards, and they float out there, in isolation. After all, you can't respond, argue, persuade, or present unless you have something interesting to respond to or argue about. Addressing standards such as these within the framework of a guiding question gives them greater purpose. Likewise, when unit activities flow from the guiding question, they won't feel like a series of disconnected tasks. For example, the common social studies standard "Students should understand the notion of balance of powers" can be translated into the guiding question *What makes a good government?* Such an inquiry might naturally spawn the following sub-questions: *What kinds of power do governments wield? What are the effects of power? How can individuals be protected from abuses of power?* We might even apply the inquiry to our local school by asking sub-questions such as *How do we balance our needs with those of others? What happens when one group imposes its beliefs on another or exercises power over others?* And, a particularly pertinent one for today: *What happens when people believe they are losing their civil rights?*

On different days or with different readings, students could be pursuing sub-questions that relate to the guiding question and that meet other standards. At any given moment, students are aware that the sub-questions they are working on connect to and inform the bigger inquiry, much like tributaries that flow into a larger river.

Let's look at another standard from earth science: "Students will identify different climate zones and their features." This can be translated to such essential questions as *What are the effects of climate on ecosystems? the development of culture? diet? How has our climate shaped how we live and work?*

Now let's turn a physical science standard into a question: "Students will be able to identify and understand the elements of an electrical circuit" can be translated to *How does electricity work?* (conceptual) or *How can we use various features of electricity to create a security system for the school?* (application)

And finally, the old warhorse language arts standard "Students will be able to identify the elements of a short story" gains traction when translated to *What makes a good story?* (conceptual) or *How can we write a good short story?* or *How does a good reader respond to a story?* (application)

Reflection Checklist

- Have I related the topic to students' past and present experiences?
- Does the topic relate to human issues and human well-being?
- How might I teach and learn collaboratively so that my students and I build a community of practice?
- How might I create a correspondence with any disciplinary communities related to the study?
- How might I bring practitioners into the classroom, either in person or through their work?
- Have I made good use of the disciplinary concepts and strategies used by practitioners?
- How might I explore the emotional, ethical, and human dimensions that relate to the topic?
- How can I remind myself to remain aware of my students' interests, ideas, disagreements, and confusions throughout the inquiry?
- How can we share students' ideas, work, and talk as widely as possible?

(see Beck and Kosnick, 2004)

Notice that reframing the standards as essential questions requires that the teaching and learning move from topical coverage to topical research or critical inquiry in which students interpret and apply what they have learned.

State Standards

Try this activity:

1. Grab a copy of the state standards that apply to your current teaching assignment.
2. Go through it and circle all of the verbs.
3. Consider whether the standards are oriented primarily toward lower-level thinking skills and information retrieval (e.g., recall, describe, retell) or higher-level skills (analyze, synthesize, understand, problem-solve, create, critique).
4. Now map the verbs you circled onto Bloom's taxonomy and determine whether the state standards are oriented towards lower-level or higher-order thinking skills. What do you find?

Teachers in four different demonstration and dissemination sites in four different states did this activity, and each time they were astonished to find that the state standards are written to emphasize higher-order thinking. Even the few goals and standards that could be considered lower-level are clearly included as stepping-stones meant to be achieved in the service of helping students reach higher-level goals. However much I disagree with holding students accountable through standardized tests, which cannot possibly capture what is most important about the complexity of student understanding, most of the national and state standards I have seen are quite good. They're geared toward the learning of substantive knowledge and sophisticated ways of knowing.

Final activity:
Consider the following two questions. Answering them will be a useful step toward reframing your curriculum as inquiry.

- What strategies will students need to learn to meet the goals of the standards?
- What kind of questions would provide the context for learning the required strategies and concepts?

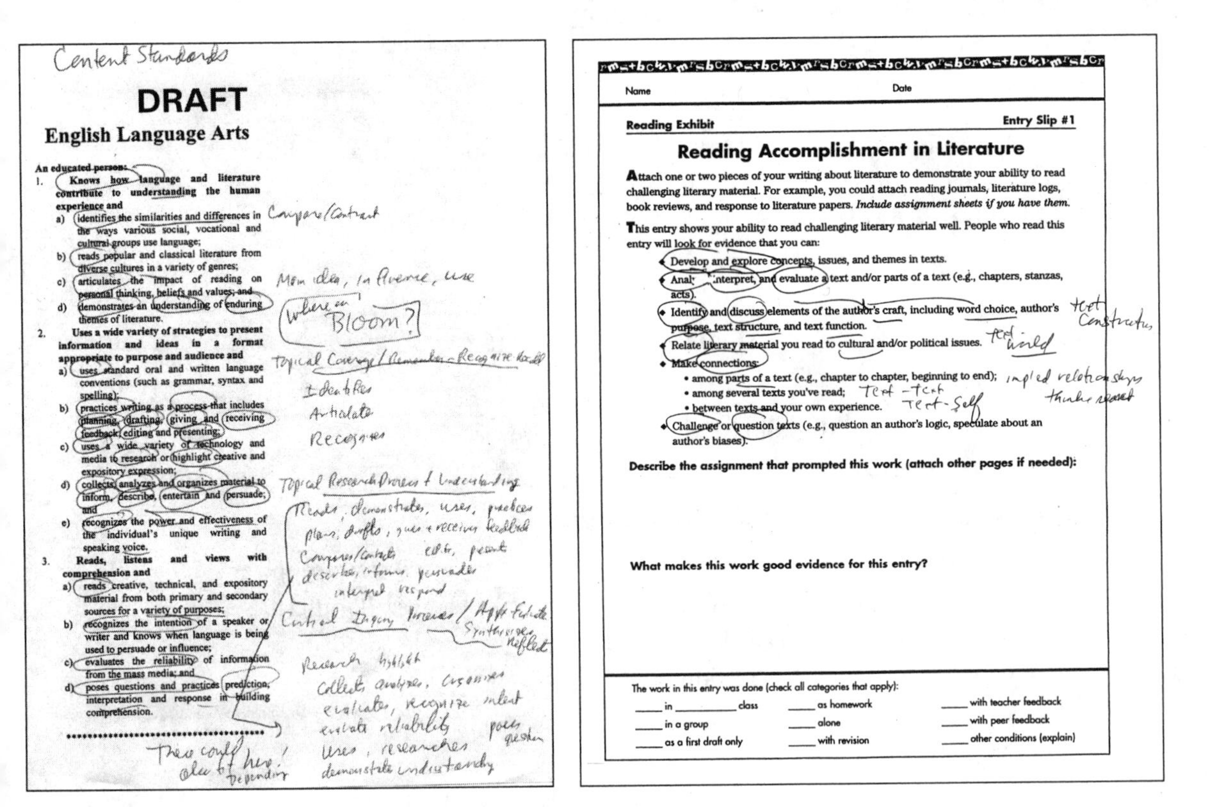

Content Standards

DRAFT

English Language Arts

An educated person:

1. **Knows how language and literature contribute to understanding the human experience and**
   a) identifies the similarities and differences in the ways various social, vocational and cultural groups use language;
   b) reads popular and classical literature from diverse cultures in a variety of genres;
   c) articulates the impact of reading on personal thinking, beliefs and values; and
   d) demonstrates an understanding of enduring themes of literature.
2. **Uses a wide variety of strategies to present information and ideas in a format appropriate to purpose and audience and**
   a) uses standard oral and written language conventions (such as grammar, syntax and spelling);
   b) practices writing as a process that includes planning, drafting, giving and receiving feedback, editing and presenting;
   c) uses a wide variety of technology and media to research or highlight creative and expository expression;
   d) collects, analyzes and organizes material to inform, describe, entertain and persuade; and
   e) recognizes the power and effectiveness of the individual's unique writing and speaking voice.
3. **Reads, listens and views with comprehension and**
   a) reads creative, technical, and expository material from both primary and secondary sources for a variety of purposes;
   b) recognizes the intention of a speaker or writer and knows when language is being used to persuade or influence;
   c) evaluates the reliability of information from the mass media; and
   d) poses questions and practices prediction, interpretation and response in building comprehension.

Compare/Contrast

Main idea, influence, use

Where is Bloom?

Topical Coverage / Remember - Recognize

Identifies
Articulate
Recognizes

Topical Research Process & Understanding

Reads, demonstrates, uses, practices plans, drafts, gives & receives feedback
Compares/contrasts, edits, present
describes, informs, persuades
interpret, respond

Critical Inquiry Process / Apply, Evaluate
Synthesize, Reflect

Research, highlight
Collect, analyze, organize
evaluate, recognize intent
evaluate reliability, poses question
Uses, researches
demonstrate understanding

These could also be here! Depending

Name　　Date

Reading Exhibit　　**Entry Slip #1**

Reading Accomplishment in Literature

Attach one or two pieces of your writing about literature to demonstrate your ability to read challenging literary material. For example, you could attach reading journals, literature logs, book reviews, and response to literature papers. *Include assignment sheets if you have them.*

This entry shows your ability to read challenging literary material well. People who read this entry will look for evidence that you can:

- Develop and explore concepts, issues, and themes in texts.
- Analyze, interpret, and evaluate a text and/or parts of a text (e.g., chapters, stanzas, acts).
- Identify and discuss elements of the author's craft, including word choice, author's purpose, text structure, and text function. — Text Construction
- Relate literary material you read to cultural and/or political issues. — Text-World
- Make connections:
  - among parts of a text (e.g., chapter to chapter, beginning to end); — implied relationships
  - among several texts you've read; — Text-Text
  - between texts and your own experience. — Text-Self
- Challenge or question texts (e.g., question an author's logic, speculate about an author's biases).

Describe the assignment that prompted this work (attach other pages if needed):

What makes this work good evidence for this entry?

The work in this entry was done (check all categories that apply):

____ in ________ class	____ as homework	____ with teacher feedback
____ in a group	____ alone	____ with peer feedback
____ as a first draft only	____ with revision	____ other conditions (explain)

Teachers circle the verbs on standards documents—and discover that they are "inquiry friendly." The higher-order thinking the standards call for is best met through inquiry.

Group 2

Standards Analysis

Low (coverage factual)	Identify? Discuss? → facts really nothing here
Middle (uncoverage) (interpretive)	Identify & Define & discuss craft, structure, function, choice Develop and explore　question Analyze + interpret (existing texts/data) Relate/Connect to Self, Other Text
Higher (Critical Inquiry)	Analyze & interpret (newly generated idea) Evaluate Relate/Connect to World - Cultural & political issues
Evaluative - Applicative	Challenge, question biases, logic i.e. adapt & resist

Ten More Tips for Generating Guiding Questions

There are many ways for teachers to reframe existing curricula with guiding questions (see also Smith & Wilhelm, 2006). Here are ten tips that will help you write terrific essential questions.

TIP: Reframe a required standard, topic, or text so it matters.

Ask yourself: Why was this considered important enough to be in the curriculum or to be a standard? What human problems/issues/questions does it address? If you have trouble answering, see if you find a different way into the topic so that it has energy for you and your students.

Let's say you are required to teach the Civil War. If you think it's going to make your students yawn, you need to go in a side door of the topic to find how you can make it matter today to your students. You could ask: *Was the Civil War necessary?* This would help you get at sub-questions, such as *Would slavery have disappeared in an acceptable way anyway?* It will also help you get at bigger questions, such as *Is war ever necessary?* In the process students might then consider the reasons and relative merits of various justifications for warfare that could be applied to current events. You could also ask, *Why did the North win?*—which is part of a larger question: *What determines who wins wars (or other kinds of conflicts)?*

Or let's say you love a particular book. Take the time to figure out why. Ask yourself: Why do I care so deeply about teaching this? Use your answer to pursue the next question: What other things can I teach with it? For example, I love the novel *Bud, Not Buddy* (Curtis, 1999) and want to use it with my fifth graders. But what essential question might I link it to? How about *Where do we belong?* since the story involves an orphan looking for his extended family. Likewise, for *Spite Fences* (Krisher, 1994), a popular book in middle school social studies book that explores violations of civil rights, I could ask, *What can we do when our civil rights are threatened?*

TIP: Consider the heart of the matter.

Brainstorm what is most essential for students to know, understand, and have the ability to do when they have completed a particular unit. For instance, standards documents in language arts often require that students should understand the basic elements of story structure such as character, plot, and setting. Typically, teachers will define these elements as terms, and students will repeat the information on a test. This process can hardly be said to be working toward understanding the heart of the matter about character, plot, or setting.

But let's say we do consider the heart of the matter when it comes to character. In narrative (as in life) character is defined by a person's responses to the problems with which she is faced. *How do people reveal their essential character?* is a question that would get at the essence of character and plot. (A sub-question may be *How does Bud—or Huck Finn or another character—reveal his essential character?*) Likewise, *How does setting influence and limit character action?* would get at the heart of the matter of how setting, character, and plot interact. It also makes "setting" or "context" an enlivened and useful concept for thinking not only about stories but about our own lives. (A bigger version of this question could be: *How does our culture shape and limit our beliefs and actions?*)

You can see that effective guiding questions are rich and multilayered. They require extended learning to answer them. Their scope can easily be made bigger or smaller as the situation requires.

TIP: Look around the community.

Think about links to the curriculum in the community or region where you work. What is in the news and on people's minds? For example, I have taught in school districts that experienced influxes of immigrants from Somalia, Bosnia, and even New Orleans due to drought, warfare, flooding, and other problems in those places. Framing a unit around the question *What is our responsibility to those in trouble/less fortunate/less powerful?* can help engage students in units on immigration, civil rights, work conditions, and many other topics. It can also help students consider the nature of "right action" in their own lives.

TIP: Consider the principal organizing questions of the discipline you are studying.

Historians ask such questions as *Who can help me tell the story of this event or historical period? Who has been privileged to tell the story first? Whose accounts and artifacts might I seek out to gain different perspectives? What do the novelists of that era communicate that historical and journalistic accounts may not? Are there voices that we do not hear when we study an event or historical trend and why is this so?* Pursuing such questions helps students to read and think like historians. The last of these questions, for example, might spur a critical inquiry in which students ask how we might recover suppressed voices on particular issues.

TIP: Ask questions like those practitioners use to guide their own work.

I recently read an article in the *New York Times* that reported on new evidence that a pregnant woman and fetus compete for nutrients, even compete for survival. The scientist's research has for years been guided by the question, *What is the relationship of the fetus to the mother's body?* The hypothesis ran counter to the conventional wisdom, but now evidence is mounting that it is right. Think of Barry J. Marshall and J. Robin Warren, the scientists who won the Nobel Prize for physiology and medicine in 2005 for their discovery that ulcers are not punishment for stressed-out, type-A personalities after all—but are caused by a bacterium. What questions might they have posed to create this knowledge? In the wake of the Hurricane Katrina tragedy, sociologists, criminologists, and politicians generated an array of questions to pursue within their disciplines. When you look at your curriculum, challenge yourself to see it from the perch of a practitioner. In fact, practitioners are surprisingly accessible and happy to participate. Go ahead and Google! There are many organizations and Web sites through which you can find experts and got their advice.

TIP: Ask questions about quality that require students to make judgments.

Questions about quality involve students in making evaluations. They may involve such concepts as *good, great, best, influential, important, successful,* and *superior.*

A unit I teach on relationships provides an example: *What makes a good relationship?* This could be easily reframed into further questions: *What personal qualities/kind of person would make the best friend/romantic partner/community member?*

In a survival unit, questions such as these require judgment: *What would be the most important adaptations that would allow a human to survive on Mars? What adaptations will be most important to surviving on the planet Earth when its biodiversity has been halved?* Questions for a civil rights unit that require students to make assessments include *What is the most effective way to promote civil rights? What have been the most important contributions to civil rights and why? Who are/have been the most important civil rights leaders and why?*

For social studies units, one could ask: *What makes a great person/leader? What makes an influential historical figure? What is the best community? What is good government?* In health, judgment questions like these could be used: *What is healthy teen living? What is the best and most nutritious diet for a teenager? What makes a good household?*

TIP: Ask ethical or moral questions that require judgment about particular concepts, issues or the pursuit of particular kinds of knowledge.

Questions that require judgment might include *What knowledge should we pursue? How should we use particular kinds of knowledge? What would be a misuse of knowledge?* For example, *Is it ever right to resist an established government? Are there conditions under which it is permissible to lie, steal, or cheat? What are the costs and benefits of nuclear power? Should we allow stem-cell research? What are the costs and benefits of cloning? Should middle-school students be required to take home economics?* Questions of this type often make use of such concepts as "allowing and restricting" or "costs and benefits."

TIP: Ask questions of application.

Remember that most human knowledge is contended because of its socially constructed nature. But some types of knowledge are not as controversial as others. These enjoy wide agreement, or they just don't provoke an emotional response. This is often true in math, and sometimes in science. For such material, guiding questions can ask about the uses, most effective uses, or misuses of the knowledge. Students can be asked, *We know this, but so what? What problems can we apply this to? What issues can we address with this knowledge?*

For example, in math: *How can we use what we know about math to build a doghouse and play area?* (I did this one with fourth graders.) *What geometry concepts would be essential to build a new gymnasium, including the ordering of materials?* For the relationship unit: *How can we create a useful friendship contract (or prenuptial agreement) based on what we believe about good relationships?* In social studies: *If we were on a deserted island, how could we use what we know about good government to organize ourselves?* For the survival unit: *How should we use what we know about survival to guide choices we make in everyday living?* In physics: *How can we create the best device for seeing in the dark?* or *How can we create a surveillance system with what we know about electricity?*

TIP: Solicit students' help to generate a guiding question or sub-questions.

A topic can be introduced to the class and students can brainstorm their related questions and interests. For instance, teacher Diane Williams pursued a wisdom project with her students. She introduced the question, *What is wisdom?* She then asked students to brainstorm sub-questions about wisdom and self-knowledge, treatment of others, religion, morality, work, happiness, etc. These became interview questions and critical inquiry questions for their future work.

TIP: Historical periods can be reframed as inquiry by focusing on the major issues or "contact zones"—geographical and intellectual spaces of debate—of the time.

A contact zone is a contested space in which a number of parties with different perspectives contend for something they want. The American West, for example, was a contact zone for the British, French, Spanish, Americans, and Native Americans, and later for the Americans and Native Americans. An appropriate question for this contact zone might be *Was the settling of the American West morally justified?*

As another example, my national demo-site codirector, Tanya Baker, reorganized her 11th-grade American literature course with questions that were hotly debated during particular literary and historical periods. For example, in a unit on the literature of the Revolutionary period, she asked: *Is it ever acceptable to revolt against an established government?* With the subquestion: *What must we accept and what should we question and resist in our own lives?* When studying Romanticism with her class, she asked, *What is our proper relationship to nature?*

In the many years I taught Puritan literature, I never once witnessed students talking about it outside of class or applying issues from their own lives to the topic. But when Tanya taught from the question *What is worth giving everything up for?* students began to make connections to their lives. One group of boys came to class and spoke about how they had wanted to leave Maine after high school but now wondered why, what would be given up, if they might return or not, etc. Inquiry requires that students connect personally to the studied material and that they in turn connect the material to world concerns and current events. Guiding questions, as you can see from Tanya's examples help make this happen. On the next two pages, I list ideas for generating such questions.

Reframing Topics as Essential Questions

	Traditional School Subjects/Topics/Texts	Possible Reframings as Inquiry Questions
Elementary	Habitats	What makes a good home? for us? for bears? for lobsters?
	Community	How can we improve our school?
	Science	How does flight influence and change behavior (for birds, for humans)?
	Introductory Geometry	How can we use what we know about math to build a new playground? a doghouse?
Middle School/ High School Subjects	Economics	How can we best produce wealth? best provide for the needy?
	Health	What is healthy teen living? What do we need to know and do in order to be healthy?
	Industrial Arts	What makes a good house? a good bookshelf?
	Ethics	Is it ever permissible to lie? to hurt another human being? to hurt an animal?
	Math	What is the best way to figure rates of decay? to estimate materials needed to build a house? (or to do any other kind of math problem)? What geometry concepts would be essential to build a new gymnasium, including the ordering of materials?
	Chemistry and Ceramics	What is the best way to make a glaze? What do we need to know to make the best glaze?
	Civics	What is a responsible community?
	Physics/Physical Science	How can we create the best device for seeing in the dark? How can we create a surveillance system with our current knowledge of electricity? How can we make the most efficient bicycle?
	Government	What makes a good government? Is it ever right to resist an established government? If we were on a deserted island, how could we use what we know about good government to organize ourselves?
	U.S. History	Is U.S. history a history of progress? Who was our greatest leader? What makes a great leader?

From our national demo work in Utah and Maine.

	Geography	How does geography influence human culture: beliefs, eating habits, values, etc.? How does geography affect plant and animal life?
	Biology	Why do organisms die? How are we like a bacterium? What are the costs and benefits of genetic engineering? Is sex necessary?
Curricular Topics	Climate	What are the effects of climate on ecosystems, diet, the development of culture? How has our climate shaped how we live and work? How is our climate changing and why?
	Extinction/Evolution/ Dinosaurs	Who will survive?
	Civil Rights	What are civil rights and how can we best protect and promote them? What have been the most important contributions to civil rights and why? Who are/have been the most important contributors to civil rights and why?
	Electricity	How does electricity work? (conceptual) How can we use various features of electricity to create a security system for the school? (application)
	Transportation	Are cars necessary? What would be the best car/bus/train/bicycle, etc.?
	Culture	How does culture shape our view of the world? How does culture provide us with ways of seeing, and also blind us to other perspectives?
	Civil War	Is war necessary? Was the Civil War necessary? Why did the North win the Civil War?
Texts	*Romeo and Juliet*	What harms relationships? What makes a good relationship?
	Bud, Not Buddy	Where do we belong?
	The Outsiders *Into the Wild*	What are the costs and benefits of conformity and non-conformity?
Genres	Short Story	What makes a good story? (conceptual) How can we write a good short story? How does a good reader respond to a story? (application).
	Oratorical Poetry	How does rap music and its counterpart, oratorical poetry (Whitman, Ginsberg, et al.), work for/against social change?

Questions That Wither on the Vine: Common Flaws to Watch For

Even the most seasoned teachers pose essential questions that could be more effective for one reason or another. Sometimes you'll notice these flaws ahead of posing them to students—other times, their feedback lets you know it's time to re-direct. Here are some common flaws.

The question:

- requires only information retrieval. If the question does not require students to interpret data, create data, or construct new understandings, then it will lead only to information transmission and topical coverage, not topical research and critical inquiry.
- begs the question. Such questions are fake inquiry questions; students are still playing the game of "guess what the teacher already knows."
- is leading. This type of question leads students in a particular direction or toward a particular answer, indicating that the topic is not truly a contested problem that can be approached from multiple perspectives.
- is so general or generic that it is undoable, or simply too big to get a handle on.
- is so narrow and specific that it can be answered quickly, without requiring in-depth exploration.

(Source: Travers, 1998)

Enrich With Why and How

One obstacle to composing a good guiding question is that we must overcome the traditional emphases on the *what.* Many questions are directly related to concepts—but if a question overemphasizes information at the expense of conceptual tools, it can keep us from the deeper waters of true understanding. It can keep us from identifying the foundational principles that guiding questions need to get after. As David Perkins, a cognitive scientist at Harvard University, maintains, understanding is "the ability to think and act flexibly with what one knows . . . a flexible performance capability as opposed to rote recall or plugging in of answers." Adding *why* and *how,* evaluations and judgments to questions helps move them beyond simple information retrieval. Facts are important, but only if they are in service of deeper understanding.

Examples of How to Revise a Question

Following are some questions our demo-site teachers have asked, along with the problem we identified and how the question was revised.

TOPIC: **Relationships**

Original question (social studies/language arts): Where do our marriage customs come from?

Problem: It can be answered through information retrieval.

Revision: How do different cultures define good relationships, and how are particular customs designed to promote them?

Comment: Pursuing the marriage custom question in a larger context of good relationships opens up many opportunities for students to bring their own experiences to bear on the topic.

TOPIC: **Civil Rights**

Original question (social studies/language arts): How did we win the fight for civil rights?

Problem: It begs the question of whether the fight is over, and the nature of the outcome.

Revision: What are basic human rights, and how can they be secured and protected?

Comment: This question immerses students in ongoing cultural debates that can be read about in any newspaper.

TOPIC: **Survival**

Original question (science): Why is it bad that animals are going extinct?

Problem: This is a leading question.

Revision: Who will survive?

Comment: No one knows the answer to this question but there are many competing

Appealing to Students' Sense of Identity

While teaching seventh grade, my team-teaching partner, Paul Friedemann, and I found that we could cover everything listed in our social studies and language arts curricula by asking the following questions on the topics of personal identity and group responsibility.

First Quarter: Personal Identity
What do people find worth fighting for? How can I best fight for what I believe in? How does this mark my identity?

Second Quarter: Group Affiliation
What is a good relationship? How can I improve the relationships in my own life?

Third Quarter: Cultural Identity
How does culture shape what we believe and who we are? How does setting influence behavior? What are the costs and benefits of being shaped by our culture? How can we overcome the costs?

Fourth Quarter: Living Together and Civil Rights
What are civil rights and where do they come from? How can we protect and promote civil rights in our own school and community?

theories. By investigating specific cases of survival and extinction, and the various relevant theories, students come to foundational understandings of survival, symbiosis, extinction, and the like.

TOPIC: **Algebraic Functions**

Original question (math): Why is algebra important?

Problem: This is a schoolish question, and it's leading.

Revision: How do people use algebraic concepts in everyday life?

Comment: This is a question of application. It compels students to learn how algebra is put to work to solve real-world problems.

TOPIC: **Identity**

Original question (language arts): Who am I?

Problem: This question is too generic and big.

Revisions: What do I think is worth fighting for? Where do I belong?

Comment: These revisions reveal identity in focused ways that are much easier to explore and articulate.

TOPIC: **Government**

Original question (civics): How do the three branches of government work together to balance power?

Problem: This is simple information retrieval.

Revision: What makes a good government?

Comment: This question subsumes the issue of balance of power but opens the inquiry up to higher purposes and alternative models.

Step Two: Identify Final Projects

Asking a big guiding question immediately makes a unit a social project of exploration in which the students are active participants. Tell them at the start that they will be extending the shared topical inquiry into personal, small-group "critical" inquiries, so they can immediately begin to look for connections from the material to their own lived experience and the world. By letting them know what kind of projects they might complete to demonstrate their understanding, they can focus their attention on making something meaningful from what they are learning.

After framing my guiding question, but before planning my sequence of instructional activities, I identify my absolute bottom-line goals for student achievement during the unit. These goals should be enduring understandings—conceptual and procedural tools that can serve students' future work in the disciplines, their future thinking and living.

Once I have identified my goals, I brainstorm what kind of projects would demonstrate student attainment, understanding, mastery, and use of the concepts and procedures. I want them to demonstrate their learning through actual accomplishments that can be perceived by all the stakeholders: themselves, their parents, other students, other teachers, the community, board members, assessment authorities, and so on.

For example, if the guiding question of a unit is *Why did the Union win the Civil War?* the final project might be a written argument, multimedia display, or living-history museum exploring the question. To extend this to critical inquiry, students could use what they have learned to consider what factors might have led to a Confederate victory, or to explain the outcome of a different war, or even to make a prediction about who will win a current conflict. For the guiding question *What makes a good home?* the final project might be to create a living-history museum of different habitats, with students playing roles as animals and wildlife biologists. Or students could create Big Book stories about finding the right habitat from the point of view of an animal or sea creature. To extend the question into critical inquiry, students could create model habitats for creatures not studied as a class, or build their own model home or school, along with a floor plan.

Step Three: Create a Backwards Plan

Once I have identified the culminating meaningful-making projects, I am ready to plan how to help students master the tools and concepts they will need to complete them. I plan activities that will take them from where they are at the beginning of the unit to where they need to be to apply understanding.

To do this, I order the activities according to the principles of good instructional sequencing. I move my teaching:

- from the kids' current knowledge to what they need to know.
- from the "close to home" to the "further from home."
- from the visual to the nonvisual (e.g., from photos, collages, and visually supported texts to those without visual support).

- from concrete to abstract (e.g., from role-playing relationship dramas to talking about relationships in general terms).
- from shorter texts to longer ones (e.g., from cartoons and fables to short stories and poems about relationships longer pieces like *Romeo & Juliet*).
- from texts with directly stated main ideas to implied main ideas (e.g., from a *Psychology Today* article about the concept of a soulmate to novels about relationships).

As I pursue the sequence I help students build a heuristic, or problem-solving guide, for addressing the issue or using a requisite strategy featured in the instructional sequence.

For example, to create a heuristic for evaluating relationships, students need to define a good relationship, identify and classify the causes of relational problems, brainstorm solutions, and so on. Such a heuristic could be expressed through a Frayer chart defining friendship (see right), or an extended definition of a good romantic relationship that references various readings, a pre-nuptial agreement or a multimedia relationship quiz. Instruction must assist students as they define, identify grey areas and non-examples, classify and apply specific criteria for different kinds of relationships—tools they will use in their final projects. Projects can take the form of formal kinds of writing (as long as these correspond to real writing in the disciplines), multimedia composing, or social action projects.

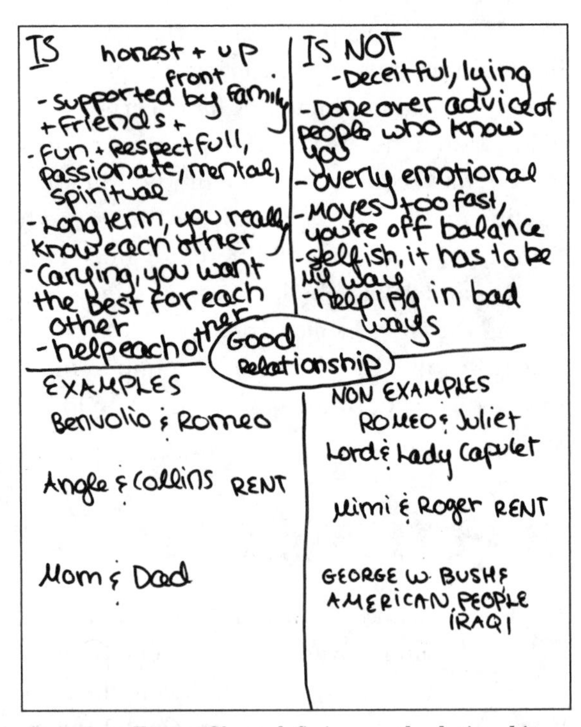

A student Frayer Chart defining good relationships using ideas from Romeo and Juliet.

Shown on page 61 is a short list of possible projects of all three kinds.

Meaningful-Making Projects		
Formal Writing	**Multimedia Compositions**	**Social Action Projects**
Arguments	Video Documentaries	Video Documentaries—Public Viewing
Extended Definition	Hypermedia Documentaries	Host Public Debate
Process Descriptions	Video How-To Guides	Volunteer Work
Classifications	Websites	Hot-Line Project
Narrative Retellings	Digital Stories	Peer Mediation Project
Fables	Multimedia Personality Profiles	Local Hero Celebrations
Stories	Digital Scrapbooks	Lake Clean-Up Project
Picture Books	Webquests	Park Clean-Up Project
Big Books	Museum Exhibits	Create/Maintain Local Museum Exhibit
Brochures	Museum Kiosks	Senior Citizen Visits
Public Service Announcements	Public Service Announcements (on video or dramatized)	Disseminate Public Service Announcements
Pamphlets	Timelines	Host/Participate in Community Meetings
Dictionaries/ Glossaries	Video Glossaries Picture Dictionaries	Present Proposals—to school board, city council, service groups
Guides	Murals	Letter-Writing Campaign
Newspapers/Articles	News Show/Talk Show	Thank-You Campaign
Poetry Book or Cycle	Dance or drama representation of concepts, processes, and applications	Informational Campaigns
How-To Guides	MTV Videos of Poems	Career Research: shadow a police officer, view medical procedures, compile interviews into manuscript.
Multigenre Research	Computer Programs	Repair or Rebuild Project: e.g. engine, engine model, cabinet, stadium steps
Case Studies	Multigenre Compositions	Waste-Free School Project
Travelogues	Public Performance: concert, recital, painting, living history museum, fashion show, meeting of minds	Physical Experience or Challenge: learn to scuba dive, run a marathon, lose weight.

An Example of an Inquiry-based Civil War Unit		
	Traditional Curriculum	**Inquiry Curriculum**
Topic	Civil War	Why did the Union win the Civil War?
Frontloading	None or Pretest	Brainstorm causes of conflict: rank those most likely to cause a war; brainstorm military advantages to be sought in warfare: rank those most likely to determine outcome.
Organization	Teacher-led; everyone does the same thing.	Teacher-guided explorations of various topics; small groups divide and take ownership of various aspects of the inquiry: distributed expertise developed around topics such as munitions, transportation, public support, propaganda, etc.
Instructional Activities	Lecture, textbook reading, worksheets	Historical simulations; drama/action strategies; small-group discussions; report out to class on small group progress; analyze data, create visual data representations, present findings and arguments to others, debate.
Questions	Factually oriented; asked by teacher	Interpretive, synthetic and applicative; students and teacher ask questions of all types.
Discussion Format	Teacher initiates; students respond; teacher evaluates.	Students bring questions to class; small group discussions; roundtable reports on small-group inquiries and feedback from class; whole-group theorizing of connections among various small-group inquiries.
Reading Materials	Textbooks, worksheets; everyone reads the same thing.	Textbook as reference; primary documents regarding industrial base, trade and trading partners, weaponry, raw materials, foreign relations, organization of armed forces, leadership and generals, transportation, economic base; diaries, e.g. *In the Eye of the Storm*; battle accounts; Internet sites; Informant Interviews, e.g., with local history buff or Civil War Roundtable; YA novels, YA nonfiction, children's books, e.g., *The Boys' War, Across Five Aprils, Pink and Say*; different groups read different texts and share what they have learned (dispersed and distributed expertise with concentrated samples).
Assessment/ Proof of Learning	Quizzes and exams, primarily of factual information	Written argument about why Union won the war, or what could have helped the South win: living history museum about the war; application of findings to a different war and a multimedia presentation of findings.
Leads to . . .	At best, some retention of factual knowledge	Apprenticeship into historical thinking; grounded theory about causes and results of warfare: ability to analyze historical data and theorize from it as a novice historian; making predictions about current and future conflicts; excitement about history!

Habitat Unit (Elementary Level)		
	Traditional Instruction	**Inquiry Oriented**
Topic	Habitats	What makes a good home?
Frontloading	None	Brainstorm what you like about your home. What renovations you would like to make and how this would improve your home?
Organization	Teacher lectures; everyone does the same thing	Teacher guided explorations of various topics; small groups divide up and take ownership of various aspects of the inquiry: distributed expertise as different groups could explore what different animals, like the lobster or black bear, need for a habitat.
Reading Materials	Textbooks, Worksheets	Textbook as reference; Internet sites; informant interviews, e.g., with local contractors, wildlife biologists; YA nonfiction; children's books, e.g., *Where the Wild Things Are*
Assessment, Proof of Learning	Quizzes, Tests	Create a living history museum of different habitats; students play roles as animals and wildlife biologists; create Big Book stories about finding the right habitat from the point of view of an animal or sea creature; create a model home and floor plan.
Leads to . . .	At best, some retention of factual knowledge	Apprenticeship into biological thinking: grounded theory about needs of different creatures for survival. Ability to compare and contrast habitats and different life forms they would support, to compare human needs to those of other creatures. Ability to see how changing an environment would change the life in that ecosystem. Interest, excitement about wildlife biology!

From Frontloading to Gateway Activities

Another way of conceptualizing my planning is to start with initial frontloading/prereading or prewriting activities that activate students' current background knowledge, then think about the guiding question and motivate them to pursue it. Next, move to gateway activities (so-called because they provide a point of entry to new learning performances) that assist students in building new knowledge and strategies. These will help them do the readings and work during the unit that will lead them to the point where they can effectively complete the final projects. This sequence must take students through a series of new tasks that will help them achieve new understandings and do new work that was previously unattainable to them. *The people who are talking, discussing, thinking, struggling, and using new ideas and tools are the ones who are learning*. John Goodlad famously said that school is a place "where young people go to watch old people work." In inquiry, teacher's work is in service of helping students do their own work and that of the discipline. I tell my students, "I already passed seventh grade. Now it's your turn!" The teacher is there to help students do the work, not to do the work for them, as so often is the case.

Example of an Inquiry Unit: What Makes a Good Relationship?

(or How I Teach *Romeo and Juliet* Now!)

omeo and Juliet is a standard requirement of the ninth-grade curriculum. I have taught it off and on for more than 20 years as a great work of literature. Funny thing is, until I changed my methodology, my students never danced in the aisles or flushed with excitement over dear William's words. In fact, they would often refuse to read it, or give up in frustration and declare that it was boring. Some would sneak off and read Cliff's Notes or Spark Notes.

I marched on, chalking up their resistance to "kids these days," I guess. I'd plow through the play from beginning to end, like some kind of salesman pitching a product, with me often explicating the play line-by-line and scene-by-scene for my students.

The tide turned when I began to reframe my teaching units around essential questions. In fact, this changed *everything*; I can hardly describe the improvement that occurred in my motivation, my instructional sequences, and my students' interest in learning.

I frame the text or topic as an essential question.

When I started teaching *Romeo and Juliet* to pursue the questions: *What is a good relationship? or What factors ruin or threaten relationships?* my young charges took notice. Even if all students don't admit it, this is an interesting topic to each and every one of them. It is something they spend lots of time and energy thinking about. They already have ideas and are able to brainstorm lengthy lists of responses to each question before reading the play. It is important to their quality of life right now and to their future happiness.

And let's face it. Shakespeare didn't write his plays to torture ninth graders. We don't continue to stage his plays and make various movie versions because it's important to have the cultural literacy and cachet that quoting Shakespeare might yield. We read, study, and attend performances of *Romeo and Juliet* because Shakespeare wrote about a topic that really matters to us all and has continued to matter to us through the centuries. He writes with grace and intensity about the experience of love and other relationships (friendship, parent-child, caretaker-child, gang member to gang member, etc.), and explores the various factors that can endanger and screw up these relationships.

If this is why we have read and viewed this play over time, then this should be the focus of experiencing the play in school.

I bring my knowledge and experience to the table as a colearner, not a sole expert.

When we inquire into important issues, the kids can't play "guess what the teacher already knows." Even though I have been married 23 years, I don't have any definitive answers to these questions about relationships! And even though I know some things, the kids have had different experiences than I have had. The playing field has been leveled: the kids have knowledge to bring to bear, and their knowledge is as valid as mine. I am in no way precluded from providing my thinking and insights, but I acknowledge that there are other points of view. It will take all of us and the multiple perspectives of various authors to explore the question. We will still have to read and understand *Romeo and Juliet.* But now we will do so in service of understanding our lives and the nature of good and poor relationships in the world. We will do what is required by school, but in a way that is meaningful and "toolish" to us. And if some kids also read *Shakespeare Made Easy,* watch videos, or use other aids to experience the play, that is just fine. The important thing is not reading every line, but understanding the play well enough to engage in our common inquiry.

I engage in backwards planning.

Backwards planning is so named because you start by identifying the final projects that will demonstrate student mastery of the articulated goals. Then you plan backwards from those final projects, going back to where the students currently are and then working through the instructional sequence to provide them with the tools and concepts they need to complete the culminating projects.

I identify my goals for student achievement.

After framing my essential question, but before planning my sequence of instructional activities, I identify my absolute bottom-line goals for student achievement during the unit.

In my Relationships unit, many of my bottom-line goals are already identified by the curriculum and standards,—e.g.: students will trace character development and its meaning; students will write an argument; students will make a presentation; students will understand conventions of literature, like setting, theme, irony, etc. My job was to decide which curricular goals could be pursued and achieved during this unit. I also defined what goals would get after the heart of the matter in terms of the play and my students' interests. This is how I identified the goal of exploring the nature of good relationships and the processes, such as tracing character change and compare/contrast, that would serve in that effort.

I brainstorm ideas for final critical-inquiry projects.

After I have identified my goals, I then brainstorm what kinds of projects would demonstrate student attainment, understanding, mastery, and use of the goals. I want students' learning to be demonstrated in actual accomplishment that can be perceived by all the stakeholders: the student, parents, other students, other teachers, community, board members, assessment authorities, and so on.

Through these projects, students state their own opinions and create new knowledge about relationships. I typically provide students with multiple choices. One choice many students exercise is to create an extended definition of their personal view of a good relationship.

My students often enjoy composing a prenuptial or pre-dating agreement form for promoting a good relationship, or an interactive relationship quiz or computer game that promotes understanding of good relationships.

Over the years, I have had students create relationship role-plays to demonstrate good and bad choices in a relationship, public service announcements to promote good relationships, video documentaries about views of good relationships in different cultures or over time, etc.

The important thing is for the students to understand—from the very start of the unit—that they will create various artifacts throughout the topical inquiry, and then move into critical inquiry by creating an artifact or social action project that uses or extends what we have learned in a new and

personally relevant way. In this way, everything we do during the unit is conscious preparation for their final critical-inquiry project.

I brainstorm ideas with students for projects to work on during the unit.

At the very beginning of the unit, I let students know that they will be completing various projects, some as we read and some after we read. Here are some projects I have negotiated with students in my *Romeo and Juliet* unit:

1. **As they read:** I divide the class into small groups. These groups become video production teams. They create a video glossary and study guide for other students about how Shakespeare uses various conventions to create meaning in assigned scenes, particularly as it relates to the topic of relationships. Each group is assigned two scenes. For each scene, they create a short video that defines a literary convention or concept (identified by me), such as irony, personification, subtext, metaphor, soliloquy, fate, and so on, and show how this device is used in real-life communication. Then they summarize the assigned scene and reenact the part of the scene that uses the device. Finally, they explain how the convention or concept was used to create a meaningful experience for the audience in the context of that scene. (My thanks to Jamie Heans for developing this idea.)

2. **As they read**: Groups role-play relationship counselors. Students collect data in their journals about how Shakespeare and one assigned character (Romeo, Juliet, Friar Laurence, Capulet, Mercutio) would define a good or poor relationship. We role-play nonscripted drama discussions with the characters and a relationship counselor. We sometimes stage these as a Jerry Springer, Dr. Phil, or Oprah interview. The collected data is used in their final argument about what makes a good relationship or what messes one up. (See Wilhelm, 2003, for more on this kind of dramatic activity.)

3. **After they read**: I provide several topical research options. Most often, students write an argument about what constitutes a good relationship or about the forces that most threaten a good relationship. They use evidence from the play, other readings, and their personal experience of the world.

Students might also compose an argument about what Shakespeare believes promotes or hinders good relationships, as evidenced by the play, or they might compare and contrast the views of good relationships held by different characters with their own views.

We develop frontloading activities.

All of the steps I've described help me to see where we are going and provide a template to organize the learning they will achieve through the unit in such a way that it is usable in the culminating project. To frontload my *Romeo and Juliet* unit, I begin with the following activities:

1. **Autobiographical writing before reading.** Before we begin to read the play, I ask students to write about their own experiences. I'm starting "close to home," encouraging them to mine their personal background knowledge and experiences related to the guiding question that frames the upcoming unit. When my friend Brian White (1995) studied the use of autobiographical writing before reading, he found that writing autobiographically about the topic of a unit (which requires making personal connections to the topic) significantly increased engagement and understanding.

   Here's the autobiographical writing prompt I assign my students. We take only ten minutes to write and then use this as the basis of our first discussion:

   > *Most young people want to have dating relationships that are fun, exciting, and long-lasting. First, describe a healthy, lasting dating relationship that you've been part of or that you've observed. What does a relationship need to be like in order to grow and last? Why do some relationships seem to work well? Be specific, and remember to write about real relationships that you yourself have experienced or watched.*
   > (from Brian White, 1995)

2. **Ranking Scenarios.** I also ask students to rank different relationship scenarios. Each one refers to a text written by a different author and makes a different argument about relationships. Asking students to rank the passage proves that what makes a good relationships is debatable. Conceiving of the guiding question as an open, contested one makes learning edgier and allows students to come to their own conclusions. In addition, to rank the scenarios, students must

understand the authors' generalizations about relationships. This helps us to flesh out and complexify the ideas we discussed after the autobiographical writing.

On the following page is the handout I give to students, originally designed by my friend Michael Smith.

After students have ranked the scenarios, I ask them to meet in small groups to discuss their rankings and try to come to consensus. This requires students to articulate why they value one relationship more than another. In several years of using this ranking, I've found more students typically rank C higher than A or B. That students seem to privilege obsessive relationships makes me *really* glad that I am doing a unit on good relationships!

3 **Opinionaires**. The third and final frontloading activity I assign is an "opinionaire." An opinionaire is a kind of survey that covers different cultural attitudes towards the inquiry question. I've adapted the following from Kahn et al. (1984).

The Benefits of Opinionaires

I've done the opinionaire activity many times with both middle and high schoolers. Their comments are often hilarious. Almost all middle-school students agree that "love means never having to say you're sorry." I can't help pitying them and thinking "you poor sods!" In response to number 5, one seventh grader named Erika indicated her disagreement and then told me: "Mr. Wilhelm, I'm looking for a trainable man!" I told her: "Good luck, honey!" Even high school students almost all agree with 8 and 11, which makes me think they are lying through their teeth! When one boy heard me say I agreed with 14, he said, "I'm going to tell your wife!" I told him, "She already knows!" Another boy, Tom, upon reading my responses, reported that I was the "fogiest of the old fogies!"

I particularly like this kind of survey activity because it again highlights different cultural attitudes toward love and good romantic relationships. (You can typically get a good start on creating an opinionaire about any topic by going to *Bartlett's Familiar Quotations* or brainstorming with friends about different cultural attitudes towards the topic.)

I also like the activity because it provides a template that we can continue to return to throughout the unit to help students practice making arguments. After the readings of our initial articles, poems, and short stories, I ask students how the author or characters would respond to different statements, and how

(Continued on p. 71)

Relationship Ranking

Each of the following scenes describes a relationship. Read each scene and rank them, from the scene that describes the best love relationship (1) to the scene that describes the worst love relationship (3). Make sure you can support your opinions. You'll be sharing them in groups and then with the whole class as we discuss what makes a good relationship.

____ **A** Joseph always felt uneasy at parties, especially parties that included people from Forest View. Forest View was Elk Grove's chief rival in every sport, and Joseph and his friends had been competing against kids from Forest View for as long as he could remember. And sometimes those competitions got pretty heated. So who could blame Joseph for saying his good-byes early? As he was headed out the door, however, Joseph caught a glimpse of Sara. Even all decked out in Forest View's colors, she was, Joseph thought, the most beautiful girl he had ever seen. Bolstering up his courage, Joseph went over to say hello. And it wasn't long before he was involved in a friendly conversation with Sara and several of her friends. An hour flew by, and Joseph really did have to go home. But he felt changed. Monday at school he confided to his best friend that he was in love, and with someone from Forest View on top of it. The kidding he got was intense; he and his best friend almost got into a fight over it. But Joseph was sure. He couldn't wait to see her again. He spent all week searching to find a party that she might attend. (Refers to *Romeo and Juliet*)

____ **B** Mary and Martin have been next-door neighbors since the fifth grade, and for seven years they've walked to school together. Since high school started, though, once they got to school, they went their separate ways—Mary was an athlete and Martin a musician. But on that mile walk they shared a lot of talk about everyday events, hopes, and heartbreaks. The senior prom was approaching and neither Mary nor Martin had a date. They decided to go together. It was funny: they broached the subject on the same day, and in fact, they couldn't figure out who asked whom. The prom was great; they laughed and danced and kidded with their friends. They didn't go on an after-prom trip, though. They had decided that it would make them seem too much like a couple, and they didn't want any uncomfortableness to interfere with their friendship. That night both of them thought that the prom was one of the best dates they had ever had. It was too bad that their "real" dates never went so well. (I've written a little story called "The Friendship" that we read during the unit that matches this scene.)

____ **C** What a whirlwind of a romance, thought Amy. Ever since she had met Tom, things had been, well, fantastic. Nightly phone calls. Dinners at expensive restaurants. Gifts. She didn't mind that Tom insisted she spend all of her time with him. After all, her friends should understand, and if her grades slipped a bit, who cares? She'd always be able to get into some college. She had a bit of a twinge when he asked her not to go out for the musical, but the dozen long-stem roses made that twinge fade. What a romance! (Refers to "The Chaser" by John Collier)

Qualities of Good Love Relationships

Identify whether you agree (A) or disagree (D) with each statement. Then choose one statement that you feel particularly strongly about and write a brief comment about what in your experience of the world leads you to feel this way.

_____ **1** Love at first sight is possible.

_____ **2** Love means never having to say you're sorry.

_____ **3** It is better to have loved and lost than never to have loved at all.

_____ **4** You are never too young to fall in love.

_____ **5** You can't expect a person to change his or her habits after you enter into a relationship with him or her.

_____ **6** Love takes a lot of hard work.

_____ **7** Opposites attract.

_____ **8** If you are really in love, physical appearance doesn't matter.

_____ **9** Teenagers are capable of true love.

_____ **10** The hottest fires burn out fastest.

_____ **11** If you are really in love with someone, then you won't be attracted to someone else.

_____ **12** Love is blind.

_____ **13** If someone does not return your affection, the best thing to do is to keep trying to change his or her mind.

_____ **14** You have to work very hard at love.

_____ **15** Love is a decision that you make, not something that happens to you.

(original idea from Kahn et al., *Writing About Literature,* 1984)

---

they know this. For instance, as we read through *Romeo and Juliet,* I continually refer students to the opinionaire, asking, "What would Shakespeare say about the statement *Love means never having to say you're sorry?* Students typically respond that he would disagree—they are making a claim. When I ask, "How do you know?" they respond that "everybody dies! The Prince says 'All are punished.' Everybody in the play has something to be sorry about that was caused by love! The mistakes Romeo makes in trying to stop Mercutio's fight with Tybalt; the Nurse's mistakes in colluding with Juliet; the Friar's mistakes with the messages and poison—they were all motivated out of love!" With these responses, they are providing data for their claims. When they add explanations of how love was the root cause of all these problems, they are providing the warranting that connects the data to the claim. This extends the conceptual frontloading that activates and builds student ideas about love into a procedural frontloading that prepares the students to use the strategies of argumentation in their "meaningful-making" project.

By the end of the play, students have considerable practice citing evidence to explore authorial generalizations and character thinking. They can stake a claim, cite and warrant evidence. They understand and have practiced the procedures of basic argument and are ready to apply them.

General Tips for Creating Opinionaires

The successful opinionaire will:

- Be framed. The students will know why they are doing this, how it is tied to the inquiry, and why they should buy in to it.
- Carefully consider the texts to be read. Determine the challenges they offer students in terms of major ideas—both implicit and explicit—and procedures they will need to use, and introduce students to the foundational concepts and strategies in the opinionaire.
- Brainstorm cultural beliefs and sayings about the topic:
  - **a.** Brainstorm from different perspectives; make sure you cover stuff from different points of view, cultural and affinity groups, political perspectives.
  - **b.** Get at edgy and debatable issues—must cover the ground—and make sure you get at what will interest students.
  - **c.** Use *Bartlett's Quotations* on different themes/issues.
- Write the major ideas in quick and clear statements that students will understand and react to with a cognitive and emotional charge. Make sure they are provocative as possible!
- Ask students to read through and respond individually with agreement, disagreement or uncertainty to each statement. You might ask them to justify their responses. Ask students to share and justify their answers in small groups, then perhaps in larger groups. Ask them to reflect on what they have learned about the perspectives surrounding the issue and if there are further issues to discuss or consider.
- Use the opinionaire as the basis of debates: as a template for considering what various authors or characters would say about the statements; for discussion of how students' views on each statement are becoming stronger, or evolving or changing—and why—as they work through the unit; as a basis for writing arguments and extended definitions, etc. In other words, consider how the discussion and writing that follows from the opinionaire will help students develop particular strategies of reading or writing: e.g., to see simple or complex implied relationships, predict, make other kinds of inferences or connections, understand how to find and warrant evidence for a claim.

Option: Have different people, different ages and situations respond and then crunch the results to see pattern.

- Be inviting and fun.

Gateway Activities: Digging Deeper With Discussion

Frontloading provides the initial purpose, motivation, and background to get started with a new unit on reading. After the initial frontloading activities, we move to what I call the "gateway sequence," a series of activities that will build deeper conceptual understandings and assist students in developing new strategic capacities that are necessary for reading the central text and producing the culminating meaningful-making project. Many of these activities involve strategies to promote productive classroom discussion. I also give students progressively more complex problems to solve.

I return to the frontloading activities throughout our reading during the unit to guide discussion. So, for example, we can ask how Romeo would rank the scenarios, or what Juliet or Shakespeare would say in response to the opinionaire questions. Of course, I prompt students to explain how they know this by using evidence and warranting. The video glossary project, the relationship-counselor dramas, and other daily activities also serve to build new kinds of conceptual and strategic knowledge that help with engagement, comprehension, and preparation for the final project. I also use a variety of other ideas, like student-driven discussion techniques (see Chapter 4) and student-generated questioning schemes (see Chapter 5).

After completing these gateway activities, students have experience with conceptual knowledge as a tool for understanding, with ways of comprehending what various texts have to say about the topic, and with strategies for constructing arguments. They are now ready to pursue their final projects. The final projects allow students to meet articulated standards and have fun. For instance, when I assign iMovies as a project to pursue during the reading, students must not only understand the plot, but also how particular conventional features and concepts add to the meaning and to our enjoyment of the play. Since different groups make videos of different scenes, they have an obligation to their classmates to explicate their play and explain *how* it is constructed to make meaning. The students have tremendous fun and display incredible creativity as they make their videos. By the end of the play, we have a complete video glossary that summarizes the plot and all major literary conventions. It can easily be put on a disc as a reference and remembrance for all students. Such glossaries could obviously be created on paper, on Powerpoint, through dramatic tableaux, or through other media.

Frontloading Check Sheet

Check your frontloading activity's quality by responding to the following questions, and perhaps having a colleague or student also respond.

1. How does your activity engage and/or build the students' prior conceptual knowledge or background information regarding your unit theme?

____

____

2. How does the activity work to motivate students for reading and inquiry regarding the theme?

____

____

3. How will the frontloading activity work to organize inquiry, set purposes and consolidate learning about the theme throughout the unit? How will it help students set purposes for their reading, focus their learning, clarify what they are coming to know, and help them monitor their learning progress? How does it provide a template for future response?

____

____

4. How can you justify your frontloading in terms of existing student interests and knowledge? In other words, can you explain WHY you are certain that the frontloading activity will be motivating and successful?

____

____

Riding the Wave

I hope that you can see from this extended example how I used a guiding question, meaningful-making projects, and backwards planning to energize my teaching, make the work meaningful for students, and help my students succeed. Students are engaged and having fun as they make connections and understandings that are applicable to their lives. And my students and I have fun. I don't know the answers, and the unit changes each time I teach it. What we read, the trajectory of discussions, what kids say in their final arguments, and what they make in their final projects differs from class to class and year to year. This energizes me and makes me feel like I am surfing with my students on the crest of the future's breaking wave.

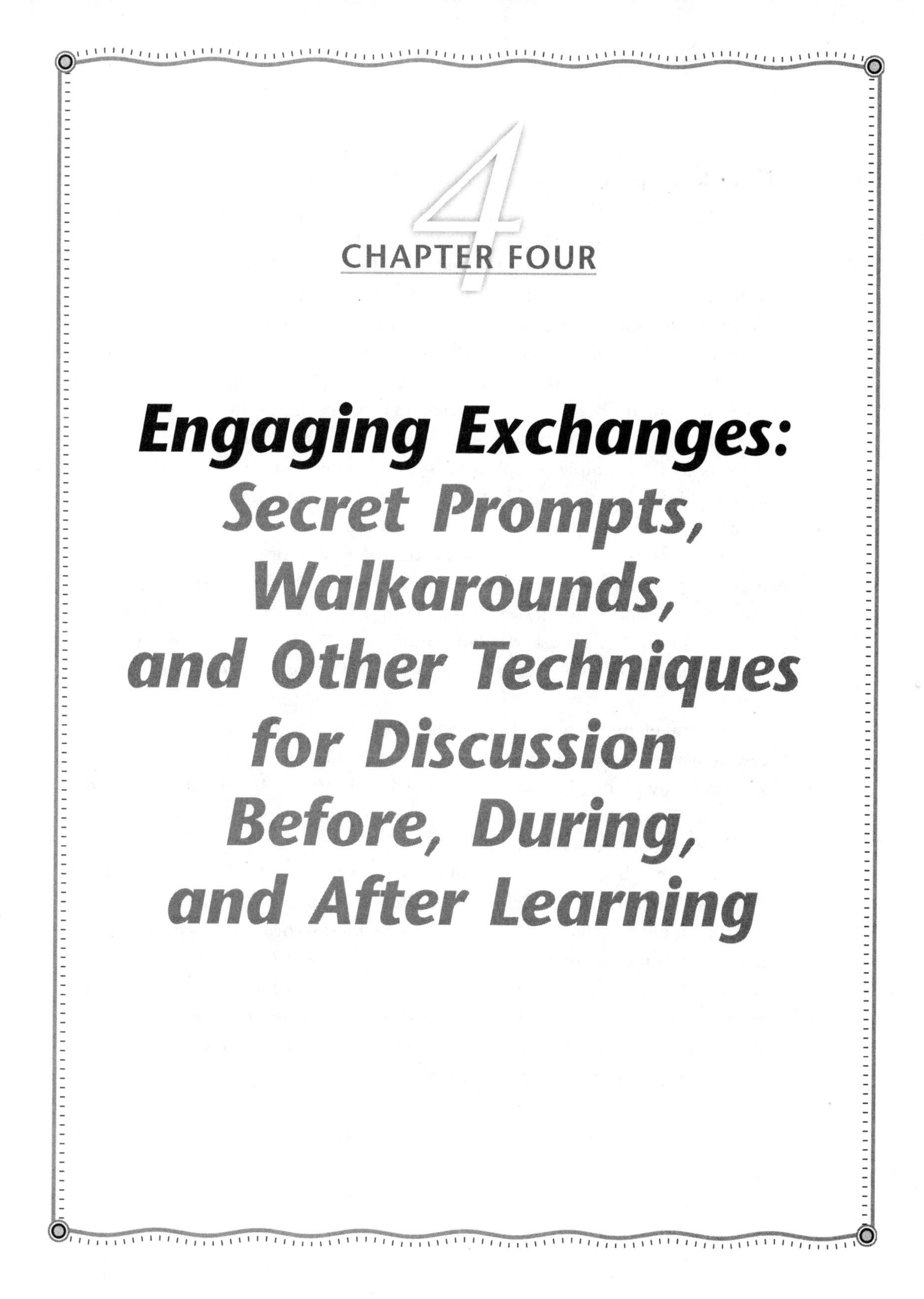

CHAPTER FOUR

Engaging Exchanges: Secret Prompts, Walkarounds, and Other Techniques for Discussion Before, During, and After Learning

Now let's explore the role of discussion in planning and pursuing inquiry units. First, I'll share another example from my work with elementary school teachers in Boise, Idaho. As you read the next several pages, notice not only how teachers anticipated and planned class discussion in the midst of their backwards planning, but also how discussion generated new, unanticipated directions for the inquiry with the discovery that the concept of "secrets" was riveting to their fourth graders.

I've been working with the Boise teachers to reframe their units to employ the inquiry method. Some of the teachers used to engage in brief topical or thematic units separate from the curriculum that the school wanted to emphasize, for example, social issues such as being kind to others. These topics would typically be addressed in town meetings or through teacher-directed lessons or reviews of school rules about behavior.

As the teachers learned about teaching through inquiry, they decided to make these social concerns part of an inquiry unit. They brainstormed several questions: *What is a good school?* (topical inquiry) and *How can we improve ours?* (critical inquiry). They asked sub-questions, such as *When do we need rules and not need rules? What is a community?* and *How can we ensure that all people feel included?*

Several elementary teachers decided to adopt the first question—*What is a good school?*— because the school is rethinking various structures and practices and there are plans to construct a new school building. In fact, they decided to organize the whole year around this question, and they took the sub-questions and turned them into units.

Once they began to implement their units, many other questions arose. For instance, when studying rules, it turned out that the fourth graders considered "secrets" a burning issue. So the teachers decided to organize some learning activities around the question, *When should secrets be kept, and when should they be revealed?* The goal was for students to write some rules for secret keeping and secret telling. Thus, the main inquiry led in this way to a mini-inquiry of intense interest to the students. Let me describe this mini-inquiry more, as it offers ample clues about the key steps in a successful planning process.

The Secrets Unit

The teachers launched the secrets unit by having students read Patricia Pollaco's picture book *The Butterfly*, based on a true story about a Frenchwoman during World War II who uses her basement as a safe house for persecuted Jewish families. To better safeguard the hidden families, she chooses not to tell her daughter, Monique.

Before the students read the book, the teachers created a frontloading activity to activate their prior knowledge about secrets—to get them thinking about the nature of secrets, and how they can be both constructive and destructive. (See more frontloading ideas on pages 68–72 and 90–91.)

Before Reading: Activating Students' Background Knowledge With Prompts

The teachers used the **secret prompts** frontloading activity (McCann et al., 2002). In this technique, the teacher provides each student with one prompt from a variety of different prompts that display contrasting attitudes toward a controversial issue. Each student is asked to read her prompt privately and to write a brief response expressing to what extent she agrees or disagrees with the statement, and why. Students can use what they have written as their starting point for an ensuing discussion. During the discussion, students can cite experiences that have informed their current stance. Students may also return the response to the teacher and revise it later after completing readings that explore the issue students were prompted to write about.

The teachers wrote and then photocopied these five secret prompts. They gave one to each student, so that each of the prompts would be received by 3 or 4 of the 18 fourth graders:

1. It is important for parents to always tell their children the truth about problems that they will encounter in their everyday lives.
2. It is important for parents to protect their children from difficult truths. Therefore, it is sometimes best for parents to tell only that part of the truth their children can handle, to change the truth, or even to tell "white lies."
3. Children are vulnerable and need to feel safe. Therefore, parents should protect their children from disturbing truths.

4 Children need to face reality. Therefore they should know all about world problems, family concerns, and community issues as soon as they are able to understand them.

5 Children should not have secrets kept from them because they might be blindsided, hurt, or unprepared if they are surprised.

The students were given about five minutes to write why they agreed or disagreed with the statement they received.

Most students felt that it was important for children to be told the truth, but some disagreed. For example, in her response to prompt 4, Julia wrote:

> I don't want to know about problems that I can't do anything about. It only makes me worry. I remember when my parents told me that we might have to move. I didn't sleep for a week. Then it turned out that we didn't have to move. I wish they had never told me since there was nothing I could do about it and all I did was worry. So you can see that I think parents should not always tell everything to their children.

As this example shows, the secret-prompt technique really stirs up students' reflections about an issue, so that they go into their reading with their fists flying, intellectually speaking. As one fourth-grade teacher commented, "This activity totally connected my students to the issues in the story by activating their background knowledge."

During Reading: Using Questions and Discussion to Engage Students

During their reading of *The Butterfly,* the class used some short drama strategies to promote talk about the text and issues pertaining to secrets. When dilemmas about telling secrets arose, the teachers often used the radio show drama discussion technique (Wilhelm, 2003).

This may be my favorite discussion technique. I start with issues from our reading. For example, I may quote a character or a statement an author has made that lends itself to debate. Or I might jump into a class discussion when students are at a point in the book where a character has a big decision to make. "What should she do?" I pose in my best radio-show host baritone. I then ask students to call in with their opinions. The radio show technique can be used to assess, attack, or defend character or authorial decisions, or to advise characters or authors. It can also be used as a way to discuss issues that have come up in current events or the school environment. Here's how to do it:

1. Select a provocative issue or dilemma from the reading.
2. Invite brainstorming and have students choose a role: Students brainstorm a personality from history, literature, or popular culture who would have a strong opinion about this issue. I encourage them to choose a role from or related to the unit of study. Students must choose a role, as they cannot call into the show as themselves. (Notice how this encourages text-to-text and text-to-world connections.)
3. Frame the radio show topic and play the host: I start the discussion in my radio voice: "Welcome to WBLAB, 101.3 on your dial! Today the topic of our discussion is . . . *Should Monique tell her mother about the ghost? Why or why not?* We are opening up our lines to hear what our listeners think! Look at those lines lighting up!"
4. Students call in to the show to voice their opinions on the topic of the day.

These are the questions we came up with as topics for one of our shows. Notice how we followed up each question about the story with another one that asked the students, in the roles they had assumed, to apply the dilemma in the story to a wider context:

- Should Monique have told her mother about the ghost? Should you ever withhold information from your parents?
- Should her mother have kept the refugees a secret from Monique? Under what conditions might parents justify not telling their children the truth about something?
- Should the girls have told Monique's mother about being seen by Monsieur Lendormy? What kinds of changes to a situation should make our previous promises null and void?
- Should Monsieur Lendormy tell the authorities about Sevrine? What should be the rules about informing authorities about suspicious activities? Does it depend on who the authorities are?

The teachers wrote the questions on the chalkboard and asked students to brainstorm characters and people from other texts, from literature, history, popular culture, our community, and so on, who might feel strongly about them. In small groups, students brainstormed possible responses for each of these people.

During the lesson on *The Butterfly*, Trace came up with these characters: "Doctor Phil, my mom, President Bush, Aslan [from the Narnia books], the Baudelaire kids [from the Lemony Snicket books], Shirley [the principal], Ms. Bauer [the teacher], the Dalai Lama [the school had attended a talk he gave], Peter Pan."

Then we proceeded to the radio show discussion. Students called in to the show as a person from their list. Their comments must represent what they think that person's point of view would be.

During Reading: Using Prompts to Encourage Critical Inquiry

As we read through the text, we used some general prompts that followed the sequence of *What?/ So what?/ Now what?* (or the sequence of past/present/ future) to help students pursue their inquiry through the story.

For example, we posed prompts that established the "what" of Polacco's story: *What are the facts of the story? What is the history behind the story?* Answering them provided students with an opportunity to establish meanings. (Or to put it another way, it grounded their understanding of what they'd read so far.)

During this early part of the unit, the teachers asked the questions, and small groups of students discussed them for approximately a minute and then compared their thinking with other groups. Later in the unit students worked in these groups to pose their own factual questions to the other groups. The asking group then evaluated the responses. For example, students posed:

- What surprises Monique when she wakes up in the night? (p. 1)
- What happens when she reveals the surprise to her mom? (p. 4)
- What happens when Monique and Sevrine stand at the window to let the butterfly go? (p. 23)

Understanding the facts of a story or a content area is of undisputed importance. But for these facts to come to life, they need to be connected to larger patterns of meaning; they need to be in the service of topical research, critical inquiry, and literacy, and they need to be functional and applicable to the world beyond the text. To work toward this goal, the teachers moved from the "What?" of the story to the "So what?," and negotiated interpretive questions about the larger implications of the story and deeper thematic meanings that could be generalized to the world.

Emphasizing the "So what?" oriented the class's thinking about the story in terms of the larger topic of inquiry about secrets. Here are some examples from the student groups:

- Why might Monique's mother respond as she does to the surprise? What might she be keeping from Monique or protecting her from? (p. 4)
- Why do Sevrine and Monique decide they must tell their secret to Monique's mother? (p. 23)

Students were also prompted to ask "Now what?" questions that provided a future orientation for evaluating and applying our understanding of secrets and how it should inform the rules we might apply to keeping and telling secrets.

- What can we tell about Monique's mother from her strong response? What might we tell about anyone who reacts this way to a surprise? How should we respond when someone reacts in a really strong way to something we say, or ignores something we say? What if that person is usually a good listener? (p. 4)
- Under what conditions might we break a promise or reveal a secret? When might the person who made us promise want us to break that promise? (p. 23)

Notice how the *What?*, *So what?*, and *Now what?* questions were all connected to a particular story event or issue. As we progressed through the book, groups of students wrote their own clusters of these question types concerning particular events and issues. They were framing, leading, and pursuing their own discussions in ways that responded to the text and also connected their life and the world to their reading.

During our debriefing for this activity, the teachers agreed that it had been successful both because it had connected the text to the students' lives and the theme of secrets and because the sequence asked them to go beyond the facts of the story to make inferences, see connections, and apply what they've learned.

After Reading: Using Techniques That Help Students Apply Their Understandings

After reading, the Boise teachers wanted students to further reflect on how the story could inform thinking about the question of when to keep and reveal secrets. Such reflection orients students toward the future, helping them transfer what they've learned to new situations.

The teachers decided to use some drama work to focus discussion. Using the drama technique of **mantle of the expert** (Heathcote & Bolton, 1995), they cast the students in the role of ethics commission members charged with drafting rules on when to keep and reveal secrets both in and outside of school. One teacher took on the role of "the stranger in role" (see Wilhelm, 2003), asking the students to summarize the story and what it might mean to the commission. This helped students review the story facts and think about deeper implications and meanings that they could use for their new task.

As the class proceeded through the unit, the students read a variety of historical texts and newspaper articles that focused in some way on keeping or telling secrets, e.g., stories of espionage and counterespionage.

The teachers prompted the students to ask and write about connection-making questions. These galvanized students to see connections between details within a text, between details in a text and those in other texts (text-to-text connections), between details in a text and their personal experience (text-to-self connections), and between details in a text and the world (text-to-world connections). We used the connection-stem idea of Harvey and Goudvis (2000) to prompt students to identify important events or issues we had read about by completing stems such as these:

- "That reminds me of . . ."
- "An experience I've had like that was . . ."
- "I remember another book with the similarity that . . ."
- "I saw a connection to this in the newspaper . . ."
- "A connection from social studies class would be . . ."

We also had students create issue trees, concept webs, picture maps, and so on, that showed the relationships of different characters and ideas.

One of the teachers wrote this response to the activity: "The great thing about the stems is that the kids are encouraged to use a particular strategy and to engage with particular ideas in the text. It almost makes it really hard for them to go off on a tangent or not do something useful! The responses led to really great discussions, too!"

The teachers also used the technique of **correspondence drama**. They had students take on the roles of Monique and Sevrine and exchange letters about the past—about their friendship before it is discovered, and their hopes and predictions for the future after Sevrine escapes. The class then used snippets of these letters to create a choral montage (Wilhelm, 2003) about the problems faced by the girls and another about their hopes and how they could be realized.

One Group's Choral Montage

Monique: I wanted to protect you, but I couldn't.

Sevrine: I know you only wanted to keep me safe.

Chorus/ ostinato: Keep the secret, and tell no one!

Monique: I did not know the danger you were in.

Sevrine: I suspected the danger, but I did not know.

Chorus/ ostinato: Keep the secret, but find one you trust!

Monique: When the butterfly was crushed by the boot, I was afraid.

Sevrine: I thought of how we were all being crushed under the boots.

Chorus/ ostinato: Keep the secret, but tell one you trust!

Monique: How could we be honest when honesty could destroy us?

Sevrine: But we had to find someone to trust and we did!

Chorus/ ostinato: Keep the secret, but tell Madame, ma Mère, who is good!

The choral montages were rehearsed, and the performances videotaped. Then the class discussed them—how they explored the themes of the story and how these related to secret keeping and secret telling.

For the culminating project at the conclusion of the unit, groups composed a final version of their rules for keeping and telling secrets. They created visual displays such as flow charts that depicted when and how a situation might change, transforming something that must be kept secret into something that must be told.

Whenever you consider a topic that touches students' lives deeply (like rules and secrets), you can be sure it will be revisited throughout the school year, whenever it comes up in students' lives or schoolwork. In this way, the present inquiry unit draws on the past as it pulls students into a future in which they continually refine their understandings.

One group's preliminary list of rules, composed after having read *The Butterfly*:

> RULES FOR SECRETS:
> Think like the other people involved—imagine you are they.
> If telling would hurt them, don't tell.
> If telling protects them or helps them, tell.
> If you are not sure, tell someone you really trust, like a parent.
> Never tell other kids, especially if the secret involves them or would hurt them or make them angry.

At the end of our *Butterfly* activities, one teacher reflected:

> This [sequence of activities] really helped them get into and think about the book, but more than that, to use the book as a way to get after the problem of secrets. It was almost like the book became a window for looking at our own lives in a way we couldn't before, and a mirror for thinking about what it would be like for us if we were in the book, and how secrets affect us now. It made the secret issue safer to talk about, think about, argue about and really get after than if we were talking about secrets from our own lives.

(My thanks to Tanya Baker for her help in creating these activities.)

Promoting Discussion Before, During, and After Reading and Learning

In the secrets unit, various discussion techniques were used to promote thinking and learning before, during, and after reading and learning. Before-reading techniques helped students set purposes, get motivated, and activate background knowledge they could use as resources to learn new things. During-reading techniques helped students inquire into the meaning of the reading and learning activities by helping them understand the literal, explicitly stated meanings, and the connections and implied patterns between various details and events. They also helped students connect the learning to their own lives and real world issues. Inquiry, after all, is all about seeing and explaining patterns. After-reading techniques helped students continue to see patterns, deepen understanding of seminal issues, and reflect on and transform their understanding, so it could be transferred to and used in future situations.

There are many wonderful prompts that can promote substantive discussion before, during, and after various activities. Following is a list of prompts we've found useful across subject areas in our national demo-site work.

Prompts to Encourage Topical Uncoverage and Critical Inquiry

Before Reading

◎ To help students activate prior knowledge, ask . . .

- What do you already know about this topic/idea/problem/issue? (brainstorming)
- What does this topic/term/concept/phrase/statement remind you of or mean to you?
- Share an artifact, photograph, film clip, chart, formula, or something else related to the topic or essential question, and ask, *What do you think this artifact means? Why is it significant? What does it have to do with our inquiry?*
- Why might learning about this problem/topic be important? How will we be able to use what we have learned?
- Describe some ways in which this problem/topic may come up in life.

◎ To promote topical research/critical inquiry and problem solving, ask . . .

- What do you already know about the topic?
- What information do you still need? How can you get it?
- What strategies will you need to use?
- What resources are available or could be developed?
- What do you think a solution or result might be? Why do you think this? Why might it be different than we expect?

During and After Reading

◎ **To make interpretive connections between ideas and applications, ask . . .**

- How does X relate to Y?
- What ideas have we learned before that might be useful in addressing this problem/reading this text/understanding this situation?
- How is this similar to another event/concept/problem/process/story you already knew about?
- What is an example of _____?
- What relationship does/might _____ have to our class/school/life/community?
- What uses of mathematics/science/history/language (related to the inquiry) did you find in the reading/in the newspaper this morning/on the news/at your home?
- Give examples of how X comes up in other situations outside this content area.

◎ **To encourage conjecture and interpretation, ask . . .**

- What would happen if _____? What would happen if not?
- Under what conditions would this explanation/strategy/principle not work?
- Do you see a pattern? How might you explain the pattern?
- How might you extrapolate the pattern? Predict the next example in the pattern?
- How might you interpolate the pattern? Predict a missing element or one between the existing elements? Elaborate on the pattern?
- What are some other possibilities we might find in the patterns?
- What insights can be reached/decisions can be made based on the data?
- What uses should/could the understandings be put to?

◎ **To help students reason across data patterns, ask . . .**

- Is that true for all cases? Explain.
- In how many ways is X similar to Y?
- In how many ways are X and Y different?
- In what ways can you tell the difference between X and Y? The similarities?
- How can you tell if this example does or doesn't belong to this category/type?

- What is the criterion or rule that would run across cases?
- What might be a counter-example?
- What assumptions are you making?
- How can you test your assumptions? How might you revise your assumptions in the face of disconfirming data?

To help students converse with an author and make collective sense of a text, ask . . .

- What does the author want us to know/believe/do?
- What do you understand the author to be saying? What would help you understand it more fully?
- What do you think about what the author said/wrote/argued? Do you agree? Why/why not? How would you embrace/resist/adapt the author's point?
- Does anyone take the same position? Does anyone have the same answer but a different way to explain it/justify it/reach it?

After Reading

To encourage multiple perspectives, evaluation, and reflection, ask . . .

- What did you find most interesting, most confusing or difficult?
- What more do you need to know about the topic?
- How did the reading help you address the problem? How did you get your answer?
- What might be another way of looking at or solving the problem?
- Does your solution seem reasonable and useful? Why or why not?
- Describe your problem-solving method to the rest of us, and why you used it, found it to be effective.
- What if you started with _____ rather than _____?
- What would happen if _____? If condition X were different?
- Describe your process/essential steps for completing this task.
- How could you use these ideas or processes to solve a current/future problem?
- Describe an obstacle you encountered and how to avoid it when pursuing a similar task.
- The next time you do this, what will you do the same? What will you do differently?

- What should the teacher do differently next year to improve learning?

To consolidate understanding, ask . . .

- What were the key points/big understandings/strategies to remember and use?
- Summarize what you have learned so that your reading buddy from a younger grade would understand.
- Why are these things important?
- If these things are true, what might follow? How might we use these understandings with other problems?
- Describe something you know/understand/can do better as a result of the lesson or unit.
- Describe how your understanding has changed.
- In what various ways could we represent and communicate our understandings?
- What kind of metaphors could we use to explain our understanding?

Question Prompts in Mathematics

Foothills teacher Heather Bauer admits that she is not a mathematician, and that math has often been her Achilles' heel as a teacher. But framing mathematics with an inquiry approach and using the kinds of prompts cited above to spur students' mathematical thinking has excited her and promoted her young charges' engagement and understanding.

She teaches a multi-age class of second and third graders. She began the year with a study of number theory, framing it with the question *What are numbers and how do they relate to the world?*

In her backwards plan, she set out to help students get to the point where they could apply various notions of numerical relationships—the golden ratio, or divine proportions, for example—to a study of paintings by several artists, including Leonardo da Vinci, and then to apply some of these principles to their own artwork.

Heather began the unit with brainstorming, simply asking the students: *What do you want to know about numbers?* Groups of students brainstormed questions. Several groups asked a variant of *Where do numbers end?* Since this was a question of general interest, Heather decided to start with a sub-inquiry into the concept of infinity, which they had studied earlier.

She asked the class: *What do you already know about infinity? How would you define it in words?* One student, Henry, answered, "I think it's like a container for numbers except the container doesn't have any sides." (Heather says this response almost caused her to fall on the floor!) Then Willie, another student, defined infinity as "an escalator that turns in on itself and you can never get off."

Heather then gave students strips of paper and asked them: *What could you do with this paper to visually show infinity?* The kids wanted to use pencils and markers, but she asked them to first do it with just the paper and tape. Three of the kids made Möbius strips (a figure eight in which one end of the strip is turned 180 degrees and joined to the first, so the strip's surface is one-sided, with no inside or outside) without even knowing what it was. One made an elongated circle. One made a figure that twisted twice and was taped. One made infinity goggles through which "you can see forever."

Next, students were asked to present explanations to the class of how their paper productions represented infinity. Many of them expressed the importance of there being no beginning and no end—this pleased Heather because many students think infinity only runs one direction. (Notice how the students are doing a kind of mini-inquiry and design with this sub-question about infinity.)

She then asked the class: *How could you use numbers, pictures, words, etc. to represent your ideas?* Some of the students wanted to draw onto their Möbius strips or other productions. Lots of kids drew spirals; one girl drew a flower with numerous petals growing out of other petals. Again they were asked to explain their representations.

The unit continued, with students studying Fibonacci cubes and sequences and theorizing about the patterns. The students were then asked to come up with their own infinite-number series and to predict what shapes these would make if they applied their series to the kind of cube relationships they had used with the Fibonacci cubes.

To conclude this part of the unit, Heather asked students: *If you had to explain what you have learned to "Six"* [an imaginary alien in their classroom who can only understand in base-six number system], *how would you explain it?*

Throughout the unit, Heather was able to support enlivened discussions that promoted deep understanding through the use of general-process question prompts. Notice that her use of general process questions made the kids do the thinking and the work. They shared, responded, and provided uptake for one another. She learned from what the students said and did in ways that informed her next question and future instruction serving the backwards plan. The questions create a context in which she was able to notice and track individual students and their current understandings. She worked through several facets of understanding as she prompted students to think and talk.

Contexts that don't allow the teacher to notice and track the learning of individual students are weak when it comes to supporting learning. Many teachers don't assess student learning until they grade a test. Why don't we assess student understanding in each activity and discussion? There are several components of normal classroom practice that make it hard to notice kids and track their learning, such as an overreliance on lecture, large-group recitation, and information-transmission curricula that require regurgitation instead of a struggle toward understanding. Heather's use of question prompts helps her notice and learn from her students, and it helps her students notice and learn from one another. Their learning journey along the backwards plan—not a lockstep march through textbook or lecture notes—is what constitutes the curriculum.

Before Reading and Learning: More Techniques to Try

There are many other techniques that invite students to engage actively with curricular material. Though each technique can be adapted for use before, during, or after reading and learning activities, I've grouped the techniques to reflect the way I most often use them.

Controversial Statements/Questions

In this frontloading technique (Kahn, Walter, & Johannessen, 1984), students are asked a set of provocative questions before they encounter a new text or problem. Before reading the play *Romeo and Juliet*, or short stories like "The Chaser" by John Collier or "The Friendship," students could address the following statements and questions for the inquiry *What makes a good relationship?*:

- *Some people believe that intense romantic feelings and attraction hinder a good relationship. In fact, some would maintain that the more intense the feelings, the worse the relationship will turn out to be. What do you think?*
- *The more intense your feelings for another person, the shorter this attraction will last. What do you think?*
- *The best romance is based on friendship.*
- *Arranged marriages are more successful than others because older people, such as your parents, know more about what makes relationships work.*

Before an inquiry on *What are the costs and benefits of technological advances?* or *Should we do everything we are capable of doing technologically and scientifically?* I presented these statements to my eighth graders:

- *The dangers of cloning, though not fully understood, are outweighed by the potential advantages for treating diseases.*
- *The dangers of genetically altered (transgenic) foods, though not fully understood, are outweighed by the potential advantages for addressing world hunger.*
- *Computers and cell phones make our lives more complicated and actually hurt our relationships and the quality of our lives.*
- *To preserve Earth, we are going to have to become less technological.*

Before our civil rights units organized around the question *What are civil rights and how can we promote them?* seventh graders entertained the following statements:

- *We should make reparations to Native Americans and African Americans for the injustices they have suffered throughout our history.*
- *Reparations are necessary to heal America's relationship with minorities we have systematically oppressed.*
- *Civil rights continue to be violated throughout America and even in our community.*

During-Reading Discussion Techniques

Silent Discussion Threads

While teaching Steinbeck's *Of Mice and Men* to ninth graders in an inquiry unit on the question *How do dreams shape and drive us?* I asked these questions about halfway through our reading: *What is most important to know about George? What is most important to know about Lennie? What is most important to know about the ranch? What reasons do George and Lennie have for both staying at the ranch and for leaving ASAP? What would you do right now if you were George?* Each of these questions relates directly to the dreams that motivate each character, and what the ranch represents for them in terms of those dreams.

To hold a silent discussion thread, I break the class up into groups and provide each student with a sheet of paper with one of the questions at the top, along with guidelines (see next page). (I give each group the same set of topics or questions, so I only have to come up with four or five good ones.) After the

Silent Discussion

How do dreams affect the people in the book?

George and Lenny are working together because of their dream to own their own ranch.

Curly's wife dreams of being a movie star + being loved and respected and that's what is always getting her in trouble. She wants to be more than she is and have more than she has.

Crooks dreams of being treated equally and being able to hang out with the guys. And having his own ranch like Lenny and George.

Candy dreams of being young & strong again.

Pass-around sheet for a silent discussion on Of Mice and Men.

students silently respond to their question, they then pass their sheets to the left and receive a sheet with a different question (and another student's response on it). I ask students to try to add something new, or a variation to the previous response. The last student in the group to receive a sheet summarizes the answers and leads further discussion on that question or topic. When that question is exhausted, they move on to the next one until all the questions have been discussed.

When I did this with my class of lower-track ninth graders, I was astonished at the quality of discussion. After a full period of engaged discussion, one of my students, Harley, had this to say: "I didn't realize that George's and Lennie's problems are like ours. They're like us and their problems are like us, too. And another thing—now I know they should get the heck out of there and I am really getting scared for them!"

Silent Discussion Thread Guidelines

1. Each member in your group will receive a sheet with one question at the top. (This could be from your teacher or from another student.)
2. Compose a response to the question. Your teacher may time you to encourage you to finish your response in one to two minutes.
3. When "time" is called, pass your sheet to the person on your left; receive a new sheet from the person on your right.
4. Read the question and response/s on the new sheet.
5. Add something new to the response to the question.
6. Pass the sheet to your left; receive a new sheet. Repeat until everyone in the group has had a chance to respond to each question.
7. After the silent discussion, a verbal discussion could be pursued, based on what you have written.

Gallery Walks/Walkarounds

This technique is a more public version of the silent discussion thread. Before discussion, students compose a question, statement, and/or visual response to a reading or issue on a large sheet of chart paper or newsprint. They can do this individually or in pairs. Half of the students post their responses on the classroom walls or seat themselves in an outward-facing circle with their responses on their desks. The other half of the class walks around to read or view each response and to chat with the student(s) who composed it. The sides then switch, with the walkers seating themselves near their responses and the responders now doing the walking. The walking students can be required to make a substantive comment or response to the work they are visiting, and write it directly on the newsprint sheet or on an accompanying sheet of notebook paper, and then initial it. In this way you can make students accountable for responding to one another. This activity constitutes a kind of small-group discussion that is "front-loaded" by the visual display on the newsprint. It can also front-load a large-group discussion, since students will have rehearsed and shared various ideas during the small-group walkaround.

The walkaround is also a good before-reading and learning activity to help students begin an inquiry topic or writing assignment. For example, when my seventh graders were planning their papers about an issue relating to civil rights as part of our inquiry *How can civil rights best be promoted and protected?* they wrote their initial research ideas on sheets of newsprint and posted them. Tom, for example, wrote that he wanted to research breaking the color barrier in baseball. Classmates walked around and

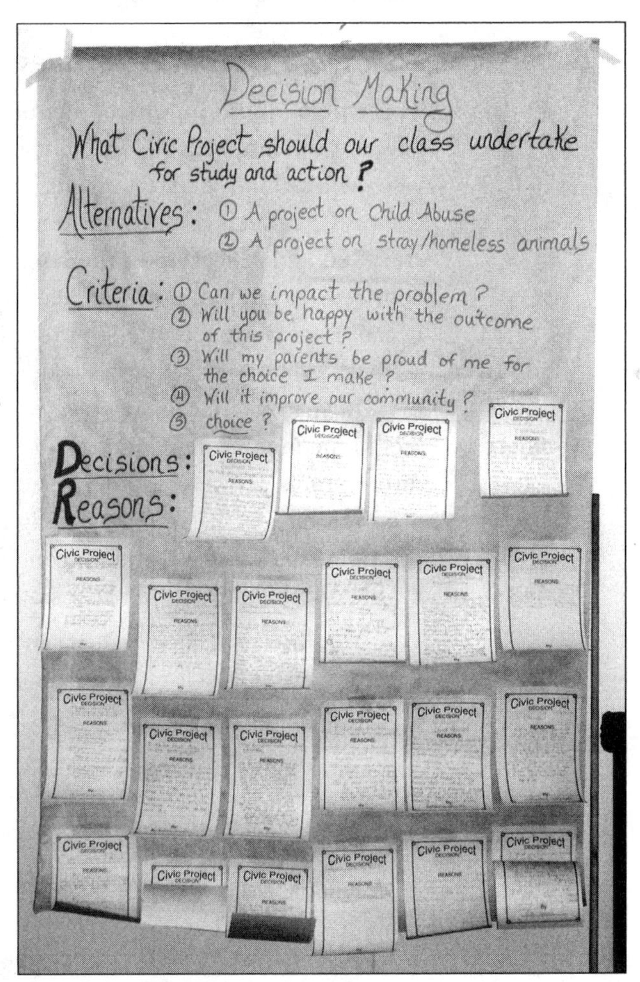

Kathy Dietrich's fifth graders post their ideas for culminating projects during a gallery walkaround, and then refer to it throughout their unit.

provided suggestions for more questions, things they'd like to know, readings and authors, information resources, and so forth on the sheet. (Alternatively, the sheets can be passed around the classroom, a variation known as "pass around." Each student gathers suggestions by passing around a sheet with his or her research idea written on it.) On his sheet, Tom received suggestions to watch the PBS series on the Negro Leagues and to read the picture book *Teammates*, a biography of Jackie Robinson; the name of a local African American man who had played in the major leagues; Web site information; and several questions students in the classroom had about the topic. He now had a wealth of ideas for "getting the stuff" he needed to write about.

Following Question (Graves, 1983) or Mirroring Question

This type of question, which encourages making connections through elaboration, is a valuable one to use and to teach students to use, since the essence of all inquiry is in making connections and elaborating patterns. The responder reflects back what the speaker has said to help both parties hear, consider, and reflect upon the comment more deeply, and then to see new connections and build more meanings in the moment. It is present oriented because it is designed to elicit more information and open up a wider dialogue so that students can see and make connections on the spot.

During our unit on *What makes a good relationship?*, I used the mirroring technique in a whole-class discussion about an article we had read on rising divorce rates. However, students can be taught to use this technique in small-group discussions as well, by having one student make a statement about a prompt or reading and then having other group members mirror it back, then having another student make a statement, and so on.

Tom: I don't think it matters if people break up or get divorced. It is their choice! It is their lives and their relationship.

Teacher: So you think that divorce doesn't matter? (*I might have also followed with: "So this means you think that both parties in a divorce typically agree upon the breakup/divorce?" or "So this means you think that divorce only affects the couple involved in the divorce?"*)

Tom: Well, it matters, but it doesn't matter as much as many other problems.

Teacher: So you think that the breakup of a marriage doesn't matter as much as other problems people may face.

Tom: Okay, it may be a big issue for the two people involved, but it's not like a national-level issue or anything. It's private.

Teacher: So you think that divorce doesn't affect other people like children, extended family, and friends?

Joe: He's got you, man! It's way bigger than we were thinking.

Teacher: So you think it's bigger than two people? In how many ways?

Tom: Ha! He got you too, man!

Entrance Tickets

I often ask students to bring in a note-card response as their ticket into the next class. It encourages them to be thinking about the topic of discussion before they come to class and to be ready to contribute. Students may be asked to write questions, statements, responses, or feelings about the reading, discussion topic, or inquiry theme. For instance, during our inquiry *What is good teen health?* we read *Chanda's Secret*, a book about AIDS in Africa. As students entered class one day, they handed me note cards with questions such as "Why did Chanda keep her problem a secret?" "Where could Chanda go for help?" "Where could Chanda go for help if she was living in Boise?" "Why didn't she tell anyone?" "Why are things so bad in Africa?" "What can we do to help people in Africa?" "How bad is the AIDS problem here?" We then used these questions as a basis for discussion. As a variation, you can always suggest or require a particular kind of response or question, or offer a comment stem or prompt, such as "An important thing I noticed was . . ." or "A connection I made to other texts we have read is . . . "

Civil Rights Unit

ENTRANCE TICKET!

YOUR NAME: JOE

SUPER STUDENTS AND READING RABBITS!
BEFORE WE BEGIN CLASS TOMORROW, I WILL COLLECT THIS SHEET! YOU MUST ANSWER ALL THREE - AS IF YOU ARE NOT ALREADY PSYCHED OUT OF YOUR MIND ABOUT OUR INQUIRY UNIT I WILL ALSO GIVE YOU A FREE QUIZ GRADE!

1) SUMMARIZE HOW WHAT YOU LEARNED YESTERDAY HELPS YOU UNDERSTAND OUR INQUIRY AND PREPARE FOR YOUR FINAL PROJECT.

2) WHAT QUESTIONS DO YOU HAVE? (MAKE THIS A THINK AND SEARCH OR AUTHOR AND ME QUESTION, IF YOU CAN!)

3) MAKE A CONNECTION BETWEEN YESTERDAY'S WORK AND ONE OF THE FOLLOWING:
A) ANOTHER IDEA FROM THIS CLASS
B) YOUR LIFE
C) THE WORLD

Joe summarizes and synthesizes his learning, with typical seventh grade personality and panache.

Note cards are also excellent to use in the midst of a discussion. You can pause discussion and ask for a summary of important ideas, a new question to be considered by the group, or a written response to a student comment or important question. You can then collect the student note cards and offer up particular comments or questions to the class. In this way, everyone gets to respond to or ask a question, but you can monitor which questions might be most fruitful to pursue as a larger group.

After-Learning Activities: Moving Toward Application

After-learning reflection should be oriented toward the future and help students transfer what they've learned to new applications. The following techniques help this to happen.

Exit Tickets

I use "exit tickets" no matter what grade level I am teaching. I like to use note cards, but notebook paper can be used as well. I ask students simply to reflect on and list the following before they leave the classroom:

- What have I learned that is important? (or: What is the most important thing I learned today? What is something I learned about our inquiry? What is a new perspective I gained? What is something I will use? How will I use something I learned today?)
- What do I want to learn more about? (What is something I have questions about/am puzzled about, etc.?)
- I wonder what would happen if _____? Something I'd like for us to do next/next time is _____. (This is a nice way to give students an opportunity to offer critiques and suggestions!)

EXIT TICKET Jasmine

I asked...
-How do you teach kids on your planet?
-Do you use textbooks also?

I uptaked...
-When Julia talked about less math I disagreed w/ her because I think that math is really important and a lot of fun. I asked why she thought that it was less important than say music.

I contributed...
By listening carefully to everybodys ideas and taking notes on what the said.

An example of an "exit ticket." This one asks the student to record her contributions to a class discussion.

When I introduce this activity to a class, I might give students only one of the questions or ask them to choose one of the three to respond to. Once we've done it a few times, students can quickly respond to all three questions.

Of course, you could ask students to provide feedback about something specific, such as to cite two to three vocabulary words that are important for the inquiry, or write a telegram to someone telling about what the text we've just read has to do with the inquiry. I sometimes use the cards as a way to promote student reflection on the quality of the discussion:

- What was good about today's discussion?

- What made this aspect of discussion so good?
- What could be better and what could make this happen?

No matter how you use exit tickets or what information you try to glean from the students, you are learning from your students what they have learned, still need to learn, and how they need to be taught. It is very easy to flip through the exit tickets in a few minutes. It's a lot better for me (and for my students) to have desires and sources of confusion shared while I can still address them. Communicating to your students that their needs drive the work of the classroom makes them partners in the dance
of learning.

I often use the exit tickets to begin a section or session of class: "Something several of you mentioned on the exit tickets was. . . . "

Survival

Roberta

EXIT TICKET

ALL RIGHT, SEVENTH GRADE PRISON INMATES!
TO RELEASE YOURSELF FROM THE CONFINES OF OUR CLASSROOM AT THE END OF THE PERIOD, RESPOND TO THE FOLLOWING PROMPTS AND GIVE YOUR TICKET TO MR. WILHELM UPON YOUR DEPARTURE!

THE MOST IMPORTANT THING I LEARNED TODAY: If you can't make a world-to-text or text to world connection then you don't get what you are reading a studying and you can't use it! I thought it was interesting to think about the bald eagle no longer being endangered when you think about the tasmanian Tiger going extinct. Text to world!

MY MOST IMPORTANT POSITIVE CONTRIBUTION TO CLASS TODAY: I asked Melinda what her take was on whether the bald eagle should no longer be endangered by law and then if people are too selfish to survive (to Mac). I listened real good + hard to their answers. I was a good, hard, caring listening friend.

OPTIONAL
ANY QUESTIONS, CONCERNS OR SOMETHING YOU'D LIKE TO CONTRIBUTE TOMORROW . . .
NO . . . YES . . . MABYE . . . YES . .
I might like to talk about my Tassie Tiger idea and how they should have had an endangered list cuz now it's lost forever and ever!

An exit ticket written during a Who Will Survive? unit.

Enactive Questions

This question type focuses students on future action (Morgan & Saxton, 1994). *What will we do now? To what new problems or issues could we apply this knowledge? What are we responsible for doing now that we understand/believe/are convinced of . . . ?* In a reading of Francine Prose's *After,* a book about how schools enact repressive social policies, we asked: *What preemptive steps does our reading of* After *make us consider to protect us from the kind of school rules enacted in that book? How can we keep this kind of situation from happening in our schools, our towns, the wider culture? How can we enact Prose's vision of how to work for justice and against prejudice in our own classroom, school, and community?*

These kinds of questions get at what is called "critical literacy," the ability to critique, resist, adapt, and use ideas to promote social action. Critical literacy questions are edgy and get at central issues of justice. Like the questions presented here, they are designed to move students from the factual and interpretive to the applicative by confronting them with a challenge that invites honest struggle and sharing. These questions clearly connect to personal and world issues that kids care about; like all good questions, they depend upon factual and interpretive questions, but they move us from the past to an immersion in the problems of the present, and to new ways of being and thinking in the future. In other words, in an inquiry context these questions promote engagement and learning and create and sustain classroom community because they are questions *that matter in the here and now and to the future of the world.*

Heuristic Questions

Heuristics have to do with developing, articulating, and using repertoires of problem-solving strategies: *What have we learned about addressing/solving this kind of problem that we can use in the future? What resources and processes are necessary to do this kind of work?* (This question type addresses the self-knowledge facet of understanding described by Wiggins and McTighe, 1998.) Such questions are good to ask after reading or learning, as they require students to reflect on learning and consolidate their learning for immediate and future use.

This kind of future-oriented question extends what students have learned into the world of functional use. It requires them to make connections between what they have just done and what they might do to transfer what they've learned to real-world issues. Addressing such questions moves students squarely into the arena of critical inquiry, evaluation, and application.

Prompts might use words such as: *apply* and *solve*; *hypothesize, induce, develop suppositions,* and *draw conclusions*; *synthesize, combine,* and *predict*; *design* and *improve*; *reflect, evaluate, judge, justify, defend,* and *assess*; *argue* and *stake a position*; *propose* and *use.*

So, for example, after a unit on civil rights, students could be asked: *How would a historian go about finding evidence of the struggle for civil rights in the history of our town? Among the Basque settlers to Boise? In Puritan New England?*

Or after our unit on survival: *What principles of survival should we remember and how can we use these principles when we buy a house/groceries/a new car? How would we evaluate our school's ability to help students "survive?" How would we evaluate our school's policies and procedures as far as environmental sustainability? What could we do better?*

After the unit on relationships: *How can we use what we have learned about good relationships to predict whether certain relationships will be long lasting? When should we decide to enter into a relationship? Given what we have learned about relationships, what would we hypothesize is the reason middle-school couples break up a lot?*

Problem Simulation/Drama Frame Questions

After reading and learning, a problem simulation that requires the application of important concepts and strategies can help student reflect on and apply what they have learned. For example, after completing the readings in our unit on relationships, I posed the following problem simulation to the class.

> The government is distressed that almost half of marriages are ending in divorce. They have hired our class to draft documents that it would like to see passed into law. We will use our readings as research documents to help us complete the following tasks:
>
> - One group is to draw up a new marriage license that sets up criteria people must meet in order to get married. *What should the criteria be in order to be able to get married?* You should be able to justify the reasoning behind each criterion.
> - Another group is to draw up a license that people must procure in order to bear and raise children. *What should the prerequisite training and criteria be for raising children?*
> - A third group is to create a prenuptial checklist and agreement for use in the public domain that will help people consider the question: *What are all the things we should think about and decide before getting married?*
> - Each person in the class is to create a guide sheet that addresses the question: *What should be looked for in a partner and in a relationship in order for that relationship to be successful, mutually fulfilling, and long lasting?* We will then see what beliefs we hold in common, in an effort to make a general guide sheet for the populace.

Critical Review Responses

One of the best ways I've found to foster after-reading reflection and judgments is to ask students to respond to critical reviews of the text they've just read. The stronger their feelings about the text, the better the activity goes—whether these feelings are positive or negative. I share a pair (or more) of opposing critical reviews of the text. (These can be found on the Internet or in various library resources and journals, or you can write your own.) Then I ask students to rank the reviews according to their level of agreement with them, or to choose one they most strongly agree or disagree with and write an explanation of why they feel as they do. They can also be asked to respond to a particular issue cited in the reviews that relates to the current inquiry or their own writing. Their responses become the starting point for discussion.

For example, Marilyne Schottenfeld gives her fourth graders several quotes from real reviews (though she could certainly create her own reviews) regarding the ending of Lloyd Alexander's *The Cat Who Wished to Be a Man* as part of her unit on the inquiry *How can we become who we want to be?*

Read the three quotes below from critical reviews of our reading:

- *New York Times:* [The book] does not so much end as disappear, leaving the reader to wonder if it isn't Lloyd Alexander rather than the wizard Stephanus who has mastered sleight-of-hand.
- *The New Yorker:* I would send any cat of mine to the knacker before I'd let him cop out in such a nitwitted way [as this book ends].
- *The Horn Book:* The author blends some of his favorite ingredients to produce a savory mixture with a satisfying ending straight from classical comedy . . . a comic and ebullient fantasy, just right for reading aloud.

Write a response to the following prompts:

- Which review do you most agree with and why?
- If you could change the ending of this book, what would your alternative ending be?
- Be prepared to justify your choice and to explain not only how your ending would change the meaning of the book, but also how it answers our inquiry question!

Sharon Zolper likes to provide several excerpts of critical reviews to books her students are reading. She gave her students five reviews when they recently read *Heroes* by Robert Cormier as part of her inquiry *What is a hero?* After the students read the reviews, she asked them to do the following:

- Read all five reviews.
- Identify a unique focus mentioned in each review.
- Find all the themes you can that run across the reviews.
- Compose three statements or questions for class discussion based on your reading of the reviews.
- Write your own review of *Heroes* and include an area of agreement and disagreement with issues raised in the five reviews.

Sharon's questions get the students to look for data patterns, an essential inquiry skill and one that prepares students for inferring complex relationships, an essential strategy for comprehending literature and data sets as will be further explored in Chapter 5.

After reading several reviews, teacher Vicki Akins asks small groups to answer the following questions:

- What comments made you think a reviewer enjoyed the book and is recommending it?
- What comments reflect a concern or criticism?
- In what ways do you agree or disagree with the comments?
- Choose the review you agree with most and the one you disagree with most. Be prepared to justify your choice during our large-group discussion.

Physical Arrangements That Promote Discussion

Carousel Seating

One seating scheme that works especially well is to form two concentric circles. The inner circle is turned out to face the outer circle so that students can discuss a question or prompt in pairs, or interview each other in role or as themselves. After two or three minutes, students in the outer circle can rotate one seat to the right so they can take up the conversation with a new person, using the insights they've already gained to fuel the new exchange. This can be done in small groups of six or eight, or in larger, whole-class groups.

Inside/Outside

A variation of carousel seating that I really like to use is called inside/outside fishbowl discussion. The students in the inner circle face inward and hold a discussion among themselves, while the students on the outside observe. I ask observing students to evaluate the participation of the student directly in front of them and the two students to either side of that student. In this way, each student is evaluated by three peers, which usually helps them pay attention and participate positively. It also reinforces to the evaluators what they should do when the two groups are flipped midway through class. I typically ask the student evaluators to focus on three or four specific discussion or listening skills during each discussion, and will shift the focus throughout the year. Here is a check sheet you can adapt as you wish.

I ask students to make a check mark each time they observe a particular behavior and also to make a short note about the contribution.

Evaluate Student Discussion				
Student Names	Added new insight	Uptake of another's comment	Specific reference to the text being discussed	Attentive listening behaviors
1.				
2.				
3.				

Procedures for Cultivating Good Discussions

Dillon (1988a, b) offers seven alternatives to teacher feedback on student contributions. These can be put on a poster and used by both students and the teacher.

The examples come from a ninth-grade discussion of Chris Crutcher's *Whale Talk* as part of an inquiry on *How can we best deal with loss?*

1. Make a simple declarative statement that comments on or complicates the student response: "Not everyone deals with loss in the same way." "There are many ways to deal with loss." "Though there are many ways to deal with loss, some are more effective than others."
2. Paraphrase what the previous speaker said: "Your point would be that his stepfather provided his own self-therapy . . ."
3. Describe your state of mind or response to the previous speaker or to the conversation so far, but be specific about what caused the response: "I really like what people said about how brutal the killing of the fawn was. But I wonder what those characters would say about why they did it." "I am confused about why you think sports aren't always an effective preparation for life's problems."
4. Prompt an elaboration or extension from the previous speaker: "Can you tell me more about why you think that . . . ?" "Can you give another example that would support your point that . . . ?" "What would a person say who disagreed with you?"

5. Ask the speaker to ask a question or ask for feedback: "What question would you like to ask us to further the conversation?" "What question could you ask that would help us further your thinking or clarify it?"

6. Invite the rest of the class to ask the speaker a question: "Let's ask John a question that would uptake his comment."

7. Provide some silent time, so that all participants have a chance to consider the previous statement.

Use Small Groups

Small groups can work wonderfully to encourage participation because they provide a less risky and intimidating environment. But for them to be effective, certain conditions must be met (see McCann, 2006).

1. Have a preset procedure for forming small groups. In my own classroom, students belong to home groups, a group of four students with whom they do daily work. A couple of times a week I have students shift into what I call rotating groups. I typically assign some of my students to develop a rotating-group scheme in which everyone works with everyone else in the class at least once during a quarter. Finally, for big projects, such as our critical inquiry projects, students apply to be in self-selected groups. I guarantee them that they will work with at least one person from the list of three they each submit. Typically, I allow them to work with the groups they apply to be in as long as all students are in a workable group. (If I am worried that a group won't work, I share my concerns with that group. If the members of the group can address my concerns to my satisfaction, I generally let the group remain. Sometimes, the members agree with me that they wouldn't be a good group and disband.)

2. Identify group meeting sites. In my classroom, students sit in their home groups. If we use rotating groups, then I tell them where to sit: "Ones sit in the back corner, Twos sit in the middle of the back . . . "

3. Always ask students to prepare something prior to group work, e.g., to bring in an artifact or write a response in a journal.

4. Start with small groups before moving to large-group discussions. In my classroom, most of the work is done in small groups of three to four students. My teacher research on groups indicates that when a

group exceeds five, everyone tends to do less. I rarely hold large group discussions except when small groups are reporting to the large group. When I do hold large-group discussions, I do so only after small-group work, so everyone has had a chance to participate.

5 Set a clear task and accountability procedure. Before small groups meet, make sure they have a problem-solving task that requires their input to do or make something(not a report that repeats previously covered information), either individually or as a group. Also, students need to know what the topic and task of the next day's discussion will be before they leave class or do a reading. They can then read the assignment purposefully and make the necessary preparations.

6 Set a time limit. I always set tight time limits for small groups to produce the response or artifact that demonstrates what they've learned. For longer projects I make sure there are daily gut checks or checkpoints to make sure everyone is making progress. I monitor progress as I walk around class. If work is going well and students seem to need more time, I can always provide it. I often find out how much more time groups need by having a member from each group show the number of minutes needed on his fingers.

7 Be fully present. When students work in groups, the teacher must be very active, monitoring and assisting student activity, but only intervening when it's needed. If you sit at your desk and grade papers, small-group work can blow up pretty quickly.

8 Have small groups report out and share what they have done. Whether they are working on a short daily assignment or a critical inquiry project, students need to know they are going to share what they have learned and produced. They need to be accountable not only to their group to get something done, but to the rest of the class. For example, when students engage in silent discussions, they know they will have to turn in their sheets with their own responses initialed. They also know that a group member will have to provide the whole class with an insight they came up with.

9 Provide for closure, reflection, and consolidation. After group work, I ask students to reflect on what they learned and how effectively the group worked together. I often ask each group to set a new "moving forward" task, such as identifying something to find out about or discuss later. I encourage students to research a question that came up and bring in their findings the next day for extra credit. I am amazed by how many students take up this offer.

Special Tips for Large-Group Discussions

Again, I recommend that large-group discussions always be preceded by small-group discussions, which should be preceded by preparatory work by individuals or pairs. In this way, everyone has had a chance to talk, and groups have had a chance to process ideas before offering them to the large group.

Remember that the way you facilitate large-group discussions provides the model for students in their small-group work. They tend to replicate what they see the teacher do (Smagorinsky & Fly, 1994).

1. Be a facilitator, not a mediator. I see my role as prompting, raising doubt, playing devil's advocate, and generally stimulating student thinking. It is often helpful to frame your own responses against the grain of the discussion: "What about looking at an opposing view, such as. . . ?" "What would someone who disagrees with you have to say?"

2. Encourage a variety of student-student interactions. For example, you might require that a student summarize the gist of the previous speaker's response before making her own contribution.

3. Encourage students not to opt out. Provide options and answer choices if a student is reticent to respond (McCann et al., 2002). For instance, you could ask a student to assess, rephrase, or respond to a previous comment.

4. Connect what the class is doing to what you have done and will do. Make explicit connections to the inquiry topic. "What would the author of the article we read yesterday say about this story about what will happen when oil runs out?" "How might this article help us write our final papers on man's proper relationship to nature?" "How might Heidi's point connect to our conversation on Monday about the dangers of nuclear energy?"

5. Don't dismiss tangents. Authentic discussion involves talking about personal issues and connections between a text and outside events.

6. Provide three kinds of wait time!

Many teachers don't realize that there are three distinct kinds of wait time. The first is the wait after a question has been posed. Waiting just a few seconds before asking for a respondent encourages everyone to consider the question. If you call on someone before asking the question, or immediately afterward, many if not most of the other students will not even think about the question. But if the question hangs in the air for a while, it is virtually impossible to ignore. If I ask you, apropos of nothing, what world-changing event happened in 1562, you will find yourself thinking about what it could possibly have been. Questions stimulate thinking if they are not answered too quickly.

The second is the wait time provided to a student once he has been asked a question. The third is the wait time after a student responds. Providing time at this point encourages the class to think about the contribution and also increases the likelihood of other students uptaking the comment.

Providing these three kinds of wait time takes conscious attention and practice, as it goes against the grain of traditional practices. But by slowing down the classroom just a little bit, student engagement and thinking can be increased exponentially.

Conclusion: Discussions, New Perspectives, and Wonderful Ideas

I was working with a fifth-grade class on an inquiry into *What is the best possible school?* The culminating project was a written proposal and presentation for the construction and running of a new school (a process the school community is currently debating). To help the students complete the project expertly, we devised a backwards plan to engage them in exploring the purposes behind various school practices and structures, and new possibilities for the way a school could be. We also knew they would need help with proposal writing, presentation skills, and architectural drawing.

To get started, we frontloaded the unit by reading some of the Professor Xargle books, in which a professor from another planet teaches his alien students about various aspects of life on Earth. His misunderstandings lead to a lot of fun but also show us how someone from outside our culture might interpret and question some of our practices. The books induce students to take an outsider perspective on things they would not normally question.

I play the role of Professor Xargle and come to interview the class about their school. Since I don't know anything about schools on Earth, they have to work hard to explain to me how things are done and organized and why. To frontload our discussion, the students make a list of what they like about school and what they think could be improved.

As class begins, the students and I sit in a circle. We begin with a short ceremony introducing me as the famous alien professor Dr. Xargle.

I begin by asking why they have a separate place for learning. Why aren't children taught at home or in the community, like on my planet? Students use think-pair-share (in which students think and write alone, then pair up and share their thinking) to discuss and rehearse how they will respond to my question. After two minutes, the student emcee of our forum calls the participants to attention and asks for responses from the pairs. Each student writes the gist of his or her response on a note card. Before responding out loud, the student hands his or her card to the emcee. This ensures some internal rehearsal before speaking. The cards, kept in order, also give us a record of the basic shape of the discussion. Everyone is asked to "spend" a card at some point during the class.

The first responder says that all Earth parents do teach at home, and some parents undertake all of their children's education at home. This leads to a long discussion about homeschooling (a direction I had not anticipated), with students talking about what gets taught at home versus school, why some children are homeschooled, what the advantages and disadvantages are, why some families don't or can't do it, and much more. In my role as Professor Xargle, I take notes and don't say a thing for more than ten minutes.

I follow up by asking how their school could incorporate some of the advantages of homeschooling into their routines. Students are given another two minutes to consult with their new partners (they turn the opposite way in the circle than they did previously). When we return to the forum discussion, the students brainstorm about bringing parents and community members into school, about doing community service projects, and about other ways of making learning in school more like learning outside of school. An open discussion ensues and lasts another 11 to 12 minutes.

Then I ask them about the weird ritual of serving strange foods during the school day. What follows is a strenuous critique of cafeteria food. I ask them what they would do to improve the cafeteria menu. They take two minutes in pairs, and the discussion opens. A suggestion that school end at noon so students could eat at home brings a huge cheer until we are reminded about the need to be in school for a certain number of hours. I follow up by asking about that, and whether recess counts as part of the required hours. Is recess part of learning? Is it necessary? The conversation takes several more weird and wonderful turns.

Five minutes before recess, we ask students to fill out exit tickets that summarize their visible and invisible contributions to learning during the class.

We conclude with a homework assignment, asking the students to write Professor Xargle a note about an aspect of school they would like to change, and how they might personally work to promote this change.

The discussion was an absolute blast, filled with both laughter and lots of really hard thinking. The classroom teacher, who had been charting student conversation turns, was amazed at the student participation and at the length of our conversation. This is what can happen when we consciously promote purposeful dialogue. It is profoundly different from the talk that dominates American classrooms. Focusing every classroom discussion on the goals of the backwards plan and using various discussion techniques to engage students in doing the work of dealing with seminal concepts and processes enlivens the classroom and promotes student understanding. Through a sequence of such work, students develop the capacity to on their own create a final project that demonstrates disciplinary concepts and is applicable to the real world. Such work makes it clear to everyone—parents, administrators, teachers, and especially to the students themselves—that students have gained a deep and lasting understanding.

Dear Professor X,

I'd like to be adopted by a family on your planet because you don't have schools, but that just aint happening. ☺ So, what I'd really like to change, is kids who don't do their homework.

I think the best way to do it would be to make school a privledge that you could loose. So like you would have to work cleaning toilets or something if you didn't turn your work in on time..

thanks

- Tarny

Dear Professor Zargle,

The most important thing to change about school, is that it is too boring. Everymorning we do 'Daily Oral Language' worksheets. They are always the same and never any fun unless you get to write on the overhead projecter. And we always read out of textbooks during science, there are lots of pictures that kind of help but its always hard to understand.

I think that we should write our own sentences for D.O.L And correct those. That way we have to learn about a subject and write and edit what we learned.

And maybe instead of reading about what clouds look like before it rains maybe we could go outside and try to identify the different kinds of clouds.

Thank you very much -

-Jasmine

Two examples of the homework letters students wrote to Professor Xargle about an aspect of school they would like to change.

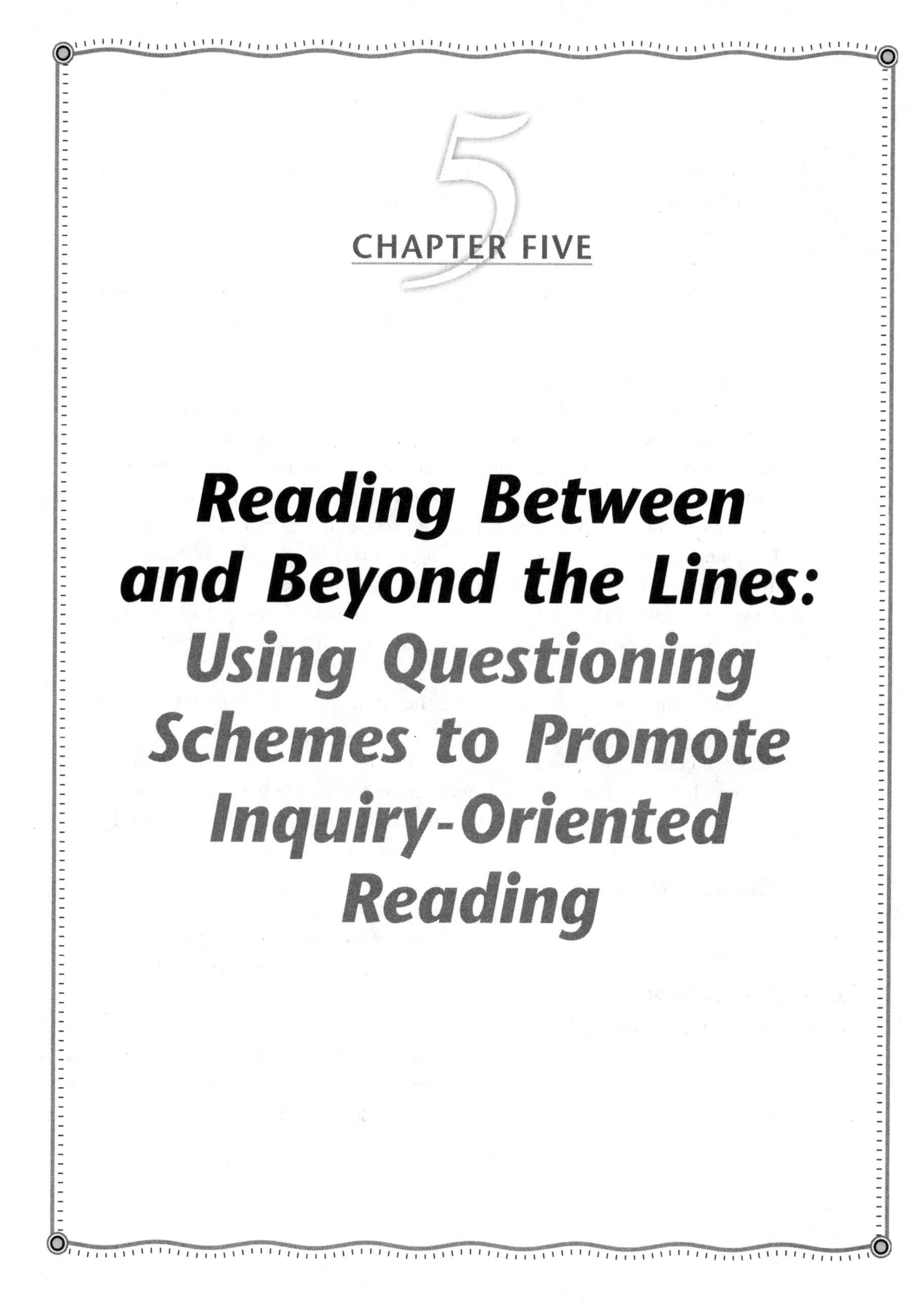

CHAPTER FIVE

Reading Between and Beyond the Lines: Using Questioning Schemes to Promote Inquiry-Oriented Reading

At the end of our unit on the inquiry question *What is healthy living for teens?* my seventh-grade students were working in pairs, responding to peers' questioning circles about books they'd read (for more on questioning-circle techniques, see page 124). After responding to one pair's questioning circle about Sharon Draper's *Tears of a Tiger* (see next page), Tom looked pensive.

I squatted by his chair. "What's up, grasshopper?" I asked.

"Just thinking," he replied. His eyes glistened with tears.

"About the book or something else?" I asked.

"Oh, about the book," he said. "I don't think I've ever thought so hard or felt so hard about a book." He took a deep breath. "We've been talking about tragic teen deaths all along, I mean, but doing the questioning circle yesterday and today really made me see that this is not just a book; this is about stuff that happens all the time, like when that high school boy Nick got hit by the train last year. And it doesn't stop, like, there are probably people like Nick's family and his girlfriend and friends who will never be the same. And it's like the event is over for most of us, but for some people it goes on forever. And maybe the people who it's over for could help the ones who it's not over for if they knew—do you see what I mean?"

"Oh yeah," I replied. "And doing the circle made you see that?"

"Yeah," Tom responded. "I hadn't really made the connection—the personal connection anyway, until I was writing the circle and responding to Trevor's [circle questions]. Then it all came home." He gave me a smile, and I gave him a pat on the back before I moved on.

As much as it's hard to witness a student face painful truths about an issue such as teen death, seeing that a book—and all the discussion around it—had deepened a student's understanding was affirming for me as a teacher. Tom would carry that book inside of him, away from this class and into the world. He would use the book as an inquirer. I was sure of it.

"Books without connection to knowledge of life are useless . . . for what should books teach but the art of living?"

—Samuel Johnson

Questioning Circle for *Tears of a Tiger*

By Sharon M. Draper

DENSE QUESTION

1. How do you think society responds to teenagers who are involved in accidents such as Andy's, where someone is killed and alcohol is involved? How *should* we respond?

2. How do you think our society/country responds to teen suicide? What could we do to demonstrate leadership in addressing this and similar problems?

WORLD AND ME

What are your reactions, feelings, and thoughts when you hear of someone your age dying in a preventable accident? (Examples: accident where someone was drinking and driving, suicide, shooting accident, etc.)

TEXT AND WORLD

Recall an incident from the news, newspaper, or history that reminds you of the accident that occurred in this story. Explain.

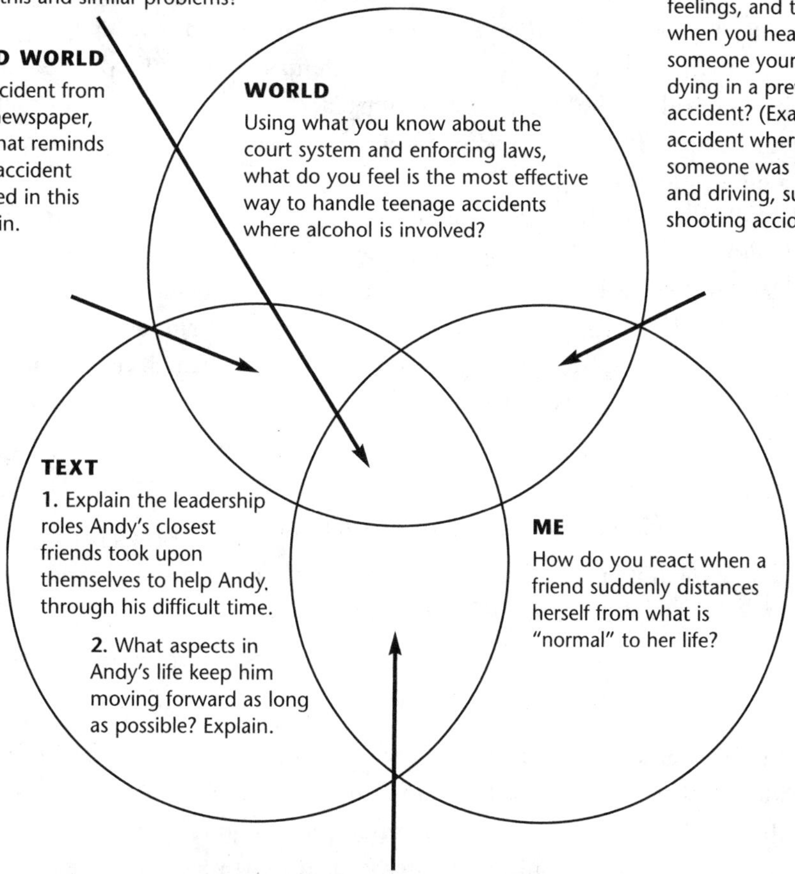

WORLD

Using what you know about the court system and enforcing laws, what do you feel is the most effective way to handle teenage accidents where alcohol is involved?

TEXT

1. Explain the leadership roles Andy's closest friends took upon themselves to help Andy through his difficult time.

2. What aspects in Andy's life keep him moving forward as long as possible? Explain.

ME

How do you react when a friend suddenly distances herself from what is "normal" to her life?

TEXT AND ME

1. Draper began the story with the newspaper article, "*Teen Basketball Star Killed in Fiery Crash.*" How would you react if you went to Hazelwood High and read that in the morning paper before having to go to school? Explain what you think your feelings, thoughts, and actions would be.

2. How would you react if you were Monty, Andy's mother, or Keisha and came home to find Andy had committed suicide? Would you blame yourself? Explain.

Using Questioning Schemes to Organize Teaching and Learning

Thus far, I've argued that we should sequence our teaching so that all the class's reading, talking, and thinking—all endeavors— progress toward application. In other words, we help students understand content and strategic processes thoroughly enough that they can look at ideas critically and then manipulate them to say or "do" something unique. Think of it as an arc of inquiry. You and your students begin in one place, ascend in understanding, and arrive in another place altogether: application, the generation of some "product," whether it is a new way of behaving, thinking or a better mousetrap.

And as Tom reminded me, the energy for this journey has to come from your students' engagement. If the content isn't framed in a way that is relevant to their lives and that resembles the way practitioners would approach it, the lessons and activities fall back to earth with a thud. Not every inquiry activity is going to bring a student to tears, but that phrase "You gotta hit them where they live" is a useful one to remember as you stride into the classroom each day.

In previous chapters, I've shown how you can achieve this aliveness with your content by:

- developing units around essential questions.
- planning backwards from meaningful student compositions and knowledge artifacts.
- devising daily lessons that help students engage in meaning-making discussions.

In this chapter, I will show you how to use questioning schemes to help connect ideas from lesson to lesson and text to text, so that each day's activities are threaded together, like beads on a necklace. In particular, we'll explore three very powerful questioning schemes that support reading, discussions about reading, and writing or meaningful making based on the reading. They are reQuest, question-answer relationships (QAR), and questioning circles.

These schemes help students:

- bring their life experiences to their studies so that the links between their lives, the content, and its applications in the world are tangible.
- notice patterns and relationships of ideas, explain them, and then infer their importance and application.

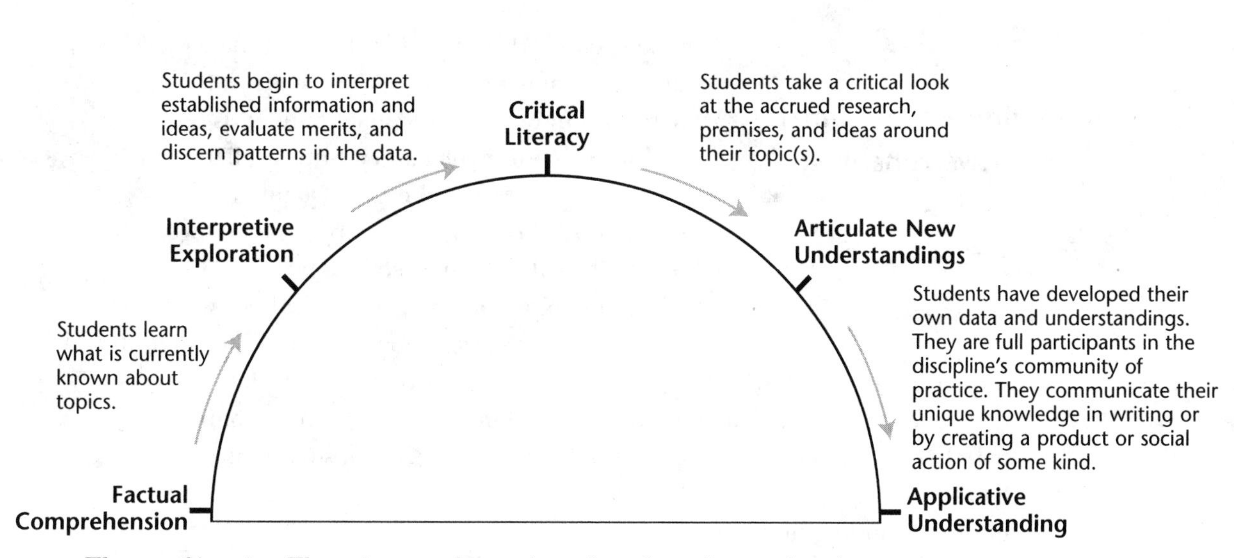

The arc of inquiry. The trajectory takes students from factual comprehension, to applicative literacy. This kind of teaching makes what we do matter—to ourselves, our students, and our world—in a way that rarely occurs in school.

- address multiple perspectives.
- pursue inquiries that focus on a single text and those that involve multiple texts and activities.
- stay on the right track—read, converse, and compose in a manner that moves their thinking from the established (past), to new understanding (present), to the possible (future).

Pattern Detecting in the World

Remember how much fun it was when you were 6 years old to do those hidden picture searches? Who knew that as you were chomping Bazooka gum and trying to spot the items in the picture, you were engaged in the kiddie version of a vital intellectual skill? Detecting patterns—noting what belongs, what doesn't, what's significant, what's not—is the essence of inquiry. To inquire is to search for patterns and infer their significance.

Point out to students that there are different types of patterns that can be detected. "Real-life" inquirers, from scientists like Stephen Hawking to anthropologists like Margaret Meade to literary critics like Harold Bloom, use their powers of pattern analysis in different ways. For example, quantitative researchers—those, say, studying the health repercussions of secondhand

"All reading should be an imaginative rehearsal for living."
—Santayana

smoke—count things so that they can analyze numerical data and apply various statistical operations in order to reveal certain kinds of relationships and explanatory patterns, like correlation or cause and effect. Qualitative researchers, who study lived experiences more holistically—like when Michael Smith and I studied the literate experiences of boys—look for what they call "themes" or repeated motifs that recur in those experiences. They identify those themes and study their relationships to other themes and phenomena so that they can make predictions about what kinds of things tend to happen together and then create interventions that can transform situations or behavior. The take-away point here is that in all inquiry, the pursuit doesn't end in understanding but in informed action.

ReQuest

ReQuest (Manzo, 1969) was the first questioning scheme to help students develop "an active, inquiring attitude." It provides a perfect introduction to how schemes can move students' thinking from the literal to the implied and then to the critical and applicative. As its name suggests, the scheme requests that we reenvision the kinds of questions we ask of a text or data set and that we follow up on—or "re-question"—the factual with more sophisticated questions that call for higher-level thinking to answer them.

The reQuest scheme involves asking students to create three different kinds of meaning while they read:

- **on the lines**—recognizing key factual information that is directly stated
- **between the lines**—making interpretive/inferential moves that require students to fill in textual gaps by making connections between various textual details or by connecting their experience to the text
- **beyond the lines**—extending thinking beyond the text's explicit and implicit meanings to evaluation and application in the larger world

To encourage these three kinds of reading moves, draw students out with question stems, provocative statements, and prompts. In the following example, students were asked to respond to statements in a reading guide. I asked them to do so before reading—and then asked them to return to it after reading.

Let's look at the guide in action. During a sixth-grade unit guided by the essential question, *Who will survive?* we read the article "The Decline of an Ancient Mariner" from *U.S. News and World Report* using the following guide:

THREE-LEVEL READING GUIDE

The Decline of an Ancient Mariner

I. ON THE LINES. Directions: Check the statements that you believe say what the author says. Sometimes the exact words are used; at other times, different words may be used. You should be able to point to one section of text that informs your response.

_____ **1** Researchers have been studying horseshoe crabs to monitor the number of breeding adults.

_____ **2** The research has determined that the loss of spawning habitat has contributed to the decline of the horseshoe crabs.

_____ **3** Fishermen are also contributing to the declining numbers of horseshoe crabs.

_____ **4** The decline of the horseshoe crab will have only a limited effect on other species.

_____ **5** Horseshoe crabs are not really crabs, but are more like a spider.

II. BETWEEN THE LINES. Directions: Check the statements that you feel represent the text's *implied meaning.* You will have to connect text information to information in other sections of this text, other texts, or your life and world knowledge.

_____ **1** The loss of a species like the horseshoe crab could have untold effects on medical progress, our ability to develop new products, and on the quality of human life.

_____ **2** The horseshoe crab's longevity shows it can adapt to many changing conditions.

_____ **3** We need to take drastic steps or the horseshoe crab is going to be in danger of extinction.

_____ **4** The world is really one ecosystem and anything that affects one environment or species will affect all others.

III. BEYOND THE LINES. Directions: Check the statements that you agree with and be ready to support your choice with ideas from the text and your own knowledge. You will need to think about the issues raised in ways that are generalized and go beyond this text to other situations in the world.

_____ **1** Human beings will only try to protect the environment when they see that their own quality of life is going to be affected.

_____ **2** Human beings have a responsibility to preserve the environment and not change it too radically.

_____ **3** Migratory birds will find something else to eat if horseshoe crab eggs continue to decline. Species must adapt to survive.

The Decline of an Ancient Mariner

A crab's bad tidings for land dwellers

By Laura Tangley

Directions: Write or draw your questions and responses on the right. Mark sections that apply to the questions in the guide.

It looks like a rusty helmet, an artifact half buried in the sand. But closer inspection reveals that this piece of ancient armor is alive, rocking slowly back and forth as the animal lays thousands of green, BB-size eggs in a hole she has excavated at the water's edge. Surrounding her, clasped to her shell or wrangling for position, several smaller males are in motion too, spewing out microscopic sperm that will fertilize the eggs. Surveying this scene on a Delaware Bay beach, marine biologist William Hall quips, "It may seem crude, but it works."

Indeed it does work, and has for some 500 million years. Horseshoe crabs and their kin, known as *xiphosurans*, or "sword-tailed animals," thrived in the world's oceans long before dinosaurs appeared on the planet. (Not really crabs, they are more closely related to spiders and scorpions.) The variety that breeds in Delaware—one of just four remaining horseshoe crab species and the only one in North America—has remained unchanged for 200 million years.

Today, however, this prehistoric creature confronts all-too-modern troubles. Since Hall began coordinating an annual springtime census for the University of Delaware's Sea Grant College Program a decade ago, the number of breeding adults on the shores of Delaware Bay—the center of the species' range and its most important spawning zone—has plummeted from 1.2 million to about 400,000. The main reasons for the decline are the loss of Atlantic beach habitat and—perhaps most significant—the crabs' value as bait for eel and conch fishermen. Though results of this year's census are not yet in, some conservationists already are worried, not just for the crab itself but also for other species, from shorebirds to humans, that depend on this living fossil for their welfare.

Horseshoe crab eggs provide a culinary bonanza for creatures ranging from young bluefish to foxes and sea turtles. In the spring, about a million migratory shorebirds fuel up on the eggs as they fly north from South America to Arctic nesting grounds, doubling or even tripling their weight in two weeks. According to the National Audubon Society's Perry Plumart, the recent crash in the bay's breeding crab population has caused declines of up to 50 percent in some of these migratory species, including red knots, sanderlings, and ruddy turnstones.

Horseshoe healing. For centuries, humans also have used horseshoe crabs as food, fertilizer, animal feed, and even weapons and tools (North American Indians attached the crabs' razor-sharp tails to the ends of sticks to fashion spears, and bailed their canoes with the animals' ample shells). But the creatures have played their most important role in medicine. Much of what is known about the human eye, for example, comes from studies of the horseshoe crab's large compound eyes. From the animals' shells, scientists have extracted chitin, a celluloselike substance now used in Japan to make sutures and dressings that break down naturally and promote healing.

In the 1950s researchers discovered that the horseshoe crab's blue, copper-rich blood contains a type of white blood cell that attaches to the toxins produced by disease-causing bacteria. Known as LAL, it is now widely used by the pharmaceutical industry to screen intravenous drugs for these bacteria. To procure LAL, a handful of companies collect and draw blood from large horseshoe crabs, returning them to the wild after 72 hours.

Medical value aside, it has mostly been bird watchers, organized through Audubon, who have had the greatest success in protecting the horseshoe crab. Over the past few years, several states, including Delaware, New Jersey, and Maryland, have set limits on how many crabs can be collected for bait. The Atlantic States Marine Fisheries Commission is considering a coastwide cap as well.

But even without official protection, some marine scientists predict the hardy horseshoe crab will endure as it always has. Noting that the Delaware Bay's breeding population has crashed and bounced back several times over the past 150 years, Carl Shaster of the Virginia Institute of Marine Science contends, "There's no evidence that the species is in danger of extinction." The real question, he adds, is whether the crab's numbers can remain strong enough to sustain the less resilient creatures that rely on this ancient survivor.

Now that you've finished the story, please comment on what you think and feel about the story as a whole. Comment in particular on how the ideas here relate to our inquiry.

After students have read and re-responded to the prompts, they can use the guide as a springboard for discussion, or for using the guide to write more examples of each kind of question. The idea behind all this discussion and modeling is to familiarize kids with the notion of questions having levels and encourage them to think of questions in those terms, whether they are posing one of their own or answering another student's.

To help students consider the level of a question or prompt, ask them: *What has to be done to answer it? What kinds of reading strategies are needed? What kind of thinking gets activated?* Sometimes it's not until we've read the text that we can see whether the knowledge required to answer a question was directly stated or implied by the text.

Use the guide as a before-reading tool

I use these kinds of guides as a frontloading activity. I have students fill one out before reading to activate their background knowledge, get them to state current positions, and alert them to key details that will be covered.

Then have students return to the guide after reading

I have students read the article and come back to the guide to update their thinking. The guide provides a great introduction to the three reQuest questions (or the four QARs, which I'll introduce in a moment) and ensures that students cover all the ground of the expert reader.

Model creating and using the schemes several times

Students need you to assist them in using guides with three or more texts before they are ready to develop them independently. And for that matter, give yourself time to become confident about using them with your students. At first it can be intimidating, but after creating a few you will become adept at it. Many of the teachers we work with have reached the point where they can create questioning schemes on the spot. To get started, use the examples shown here as models, then try creating two or three with a partner before going off to create them on your own.

Gather a panel of experts

After you and your students have worked with the guide on a few texts, it's time for them to try composing questions themselves. Select a panel of students to develop a guide to give the class for a text they've just read. Have students brainstorm questions as they skim back over the text. I have groups take turns creating the guides with different readings they all have read. For example, I might ask students to compose a three-level guide that uses all three levels of response. Students learn to classify the question types and formulate questions of each type. They also get immediate feedback from their peers on whether the questions were clear, whether their type was correctly identified, and whether they focused on key details, connections, and applications.

When I taught the survival unit the following year, I had a panel of students create their own guide for the article on horseshoe crabs. Following is what they came up with. Notice how well these sixth graders were able to ask and interrelate the different question types.

On the Lines

Why has the horseshoe crab population been declining?

What other creatures are affected by the declining crab population?

Between the Lines

Why are these other creatures affected by the declining crab population? What will happen to these other creatures if the crab population continues to decline? How is humanity probably being affected?

Beyond the Lines

How can this trend of declining population be reversed? What can we personally do to help reverse this trend? What current events and lifestyles are contributing to the plight of the crab? How will other plants and animals not mentioned in the text probably be affected by these same trends in human activity, climate, and habitat conditions? How do you feel when someone else's actions negatively affect you? How will future generations feel if we continue to contribute to this problem and do not address it? What will be hard about making the personal and social changes that will be necessary? What obstacles will we have to overcome?

Tips for Students

- Remind students to classify and sequence their questions or prompt types.
- Tell them that one question should help to answer the next one. The facts elicited by an "on the lines" question should highlight details necessary to answer a "between the lines" question. Creating these linked question chains helps students see how information leads to making interpretive connections between separate details in data sets, how interpretations lead to further knowledge, and how this knowledge leads to critical evaluation and use.
- Have them test out their questions or prompts with other students before using with the whole class.

The purpose of reQuest is to provide students with assisted practice naming different reading moves and question types and the work these kinds of questions do. Once they have mastered these skills, students will be able to use these strategies independently while reading.

ReQuest for Another Reading

For the next reading in our survival unit, we used the article "Republic of Cockroaches" written by David Quammen for *Outside* magazine. Small groups worked as panels to write the three question types. The article explored the fact that cockroaches will probably survive after all other species have perished.

One group put together this reQuest scheme based on their reading:

> **On the Lines**
> How long has the cockroach been around? How long will it be around?
>
> **Between the Lines**
> Why is the cockroach going to survive longer than human beings?
>
> **Beyond the Lines**
> What could we learn from cockroaches about ways of living that would help us survive as individuals, as groups, and as a species?

For the first reading in a unit, I typically create the guide (teacher models or teacher does/students watch and learn), and then I work with a panel of students to create the second one (teacher mentors or teacher does/students help). Next, small groups work independently on their guides (teacher monitors or students do together/teacher helps) as we read the other texts. Eventually, of course, students internalize the scheme.

QARs

One of my favorite questioning schemes is Taffy Raphael's (1984) question-answer relationships, or QAR. Raphael divides the four QAR types of questions into two categories: "in the text" questions and "in my head" questions.

In the Text Questions

Right there questions are factual, requiring students to find the spot "right there" in the text where the question is answered. They are the QAR version of reQuest's "on the lines" questions.

Think and search questions, like "between the lines" questions, are interpretive questions that require the reader to search for the various details in the text and think about the nature of the connection between the details. If details are close together, the question is easier to answer and constitutes a "simple implied relationship" question; if details are greater in number, far apart, and less obviously related, then answering the question requires more work and can be considered a "complex implied relationship" question (Hillocks, 1980).

Republic of Cockroaches

When the Ultimate Exterminator Meets the Ultimate Pest

a synopsis of a chapter in *Natural Acts* by David Quammen

In the fifth chapter of Matthew's gospel, Christ is quoted as saying that the meek shall inherit the earth, but lately, other opinions suggest that it will more likely go to the cockroaches.

A decidedly ugly prospect: That our dear planet—after the final close of all human beings—will be ravaged and overrun by great multitudes of cockroaches, plagues of them, scuttering herds shoulder to shoulder like the old herds of bison. Legions of cockroaches will sweep over the prairies like driver ants. This, unfortunately, is not the fantasy of a pessimist. It is the touch of hard, cold science.

The cockroach is a popular test subject for laboratory research. It adapts well to captivity, lives a long life, reproduces quickly, and will survive in full vigor on Purina Dog Chow. The largest American species is about two inches long. Here is an animal of frugal habits, tenacious of life, eager to live in laboratories and requiring very modest space. Tenacious of life, indeed! Not only in kitchen cupboards, but also in dark corners of the basement, the average cockroach is a hard beast to kill.

Survival. The cockroach is roughly 250 million years old, which makes it the oldest of living insects, possibly even the oldest known air-breathing animal. Think of it this way: Long before the first primitive mammal appeared on earth, before the first bird, before the first pine tree, before the first reptile, the cockroaches were running wild. They can live almost anywhere and eat almost anything.

Unlike most insects, they have mouthparts that enable them to take hard foods, soft foods, and liquids. They tend to eat anything; however, cucumbers disagree with them.

They are flattened enough to squeeze into the narrowest hiding place. They are quick on their feet, and can fly if they need to. But the real reason for their long continued success and their excellent prospects for the future is this: They have never specialized.

If there was ever to be a nuclear war, probably the cockroaches would prevail. The lethal dose for animals in a pasture is 180 rads (gamma radiation). For horses it is 350 rads. Water is a shield for radiation, so the lethal dose for fish is from 1,100 rads to 5,600. The dose for humans is not known (no one has been tested to date), but around 600 is the guess.

Cockroaches who were exposed to 830 rads lived to a ripe old age. A large test group was blasted with about 10,000 rads and *half* the group was alive two weeks later. They don't know exactly how long the second half lasted, but long enough for egg capsules to be delivered, hatch and the life cycle to continue on.

With luck maybe this won't happen. What do you suppose the common cockroach thinks of a can of Raid?

Student-Composed QAR Questions

For "Republic of Cockroaches," by David Quammen

IN THE TEXT

Right There

- How long has the cockroach been around?
- What is the major reason for the cockroaches' survival?

Think and Search

- Why is the cockroach used in many lab experiments?
- How do we know cockroaches are resilient?
- How is the cockroach more likely to survive than humans?

IN MY HEAD

Author and Me

- How is the cockroach's behavior like that of other insects, wildlife, etc.?
- If you were a cockroach, what would be your favorite meals?

On My Own

- If you had to be an insect, what kind of insect would you be?
- What are you tenacious about?
- Who is going to survive?

In My Head Questions

These two types of questions, similar to reQuest's beyond the lines questions, emphasize that the reader must make use of extra-textual information, either from the reader's experiences or the larger world.

Author and me questions require the reader to bring her own knowledge and experiences to bear on a text. The reader might have to fill in gaps in the text or extend and elaborate on what's in the text. To answer questions of this type, students must be able to combine what they know and have experienced with what's in the text.

The final question category is **on my own questions.** Answering this kind of question does not require specific information from the text (though having read the text might stimulate the student or assist her in addressing it). Inquiry questions are often questions of this type; for instance, you can tentatively answer the question of *Who will survive?* or *What makes a good relationship?* without having completed any particular reading, although readings and learning activities might help you answer it. These questions are evaluative or applicative: answers typically stake a claim about the world or suggest potential actions.

The QAR scheme is easy for students of all ages to learn and to use on their own. It emphasizes that readers must use various sources of information from their personal experience and the world as they read. It highlights that different questions require different kinds of work to answer, and that various cognitive activities go on while reading. The QAR scheme also shows that these various activities are not only okay (something students who have been taught in information-driven models may not know), but are absolutely necessary to good reading.

Using QAR With Novels

Often when I'm teaching a novel, I provide a QAR guide for each of the first few chapters. I ask the questions, and students answer them. We have the chance to discuss the question types, how the type is determined by what we have to do to answer that type, and the different uses of each type. (Modeling) For the next few chapters of the novel, I might provide a guide with one example of each QAR type and work with students in groups to help them compose additional examples of each type. (Mentoring) By the end of the book, students are composing their own QAR guides for each chapter. (I am monitoring.) They use one another's guides to foster discussion and to review.

Author and Me Question

What do you think might happen to Uncle Hammer because of his trick at the bridge?

I think the nightriders might get mad and go after Uncle Hammer.

This QAR card was composed by students during a QAR Review Game after reading Taylor's Roll of Thunder, Hear My Cry.

QAR Review Game

A great way to get students to review and use the QAR question types (or any other question type) is through a review game. After we've read a section of text, I ask small groups to create a complete set of QARs for that section. During the game, the first group asks one of their questions. The next group must identify the question type, give an acceptable answer, and demonstrate that what they did to answer the question shows they were right about the question type. If they are correct, they score a point and ask their question to the next group, and so on. If they are not correct, the third group can dispute their answer and earn the point.

The Questioning Circle

The questioning circle of Patricia Kelly and Leila Christenbury (1984) does some of the same work as reQuest and QAR by emphasizing the different resources students need to bring to bear to understand, interpret, evaluate, and use messages in text. As such, the questioning circle helps students inquire into the meaning of a single text (or data set) in ways that contribute to a larger inquiry. The questioning circle differs from reQuest and QAR in that it emphasizes that we *must* draw on and connect textual information to our personal experience and to disciplinary or world knowledge in order to truly inquire about and understand a text. As you can see in the example on page 128 (and 111), the scheme also works as a graphic organizer.

The questioning circle encourages students to ask "pure" questions that rely on one resource (either self, text, or world knowledge) and then "shaded" ones that combine knowledge from these resources. Finally, students ask "dense" questions that organize textual inquiry by combining all three sources.

As a principle of good sequencing, it can be helpful to use these schemes with children's books early in middle school and high school units. (For example, early in my unit on relationships, I often like to use Maurice Sendak's *Where the Wild Things Are.*) I also model a scheme before mentoring and monitoring. Next I have the students help me use it, and then we all work together using it. Once they've internalized it, the students use the scheme on their own. This process is easier to begin with a picture book, since such texts are usually fairly simple and comprehension is supported by the pictures, but they still operate on multiple levels. It is important to note that the purpose of using questioning schemes, as with any other strategy, is to help the students internalize and independently use the scheme. If this does not happen, the potential of the scheme is not actualized.

Following are excerpts from a classroom transcript of my introduction of the questioning circle to a group of fifth graders immediately after a reading and rereading of *Where the Wild Things Are.* In parentheses, I comment on what I am trying to achieve.

Using a Questioning Circle With Where the Wild Things Are

J.W.: All right, super students, what is our essential inquiry question for this unit? *(I remind students of the inquiry question before each lesson to lend coherence to everything we do and to encourage students to see how daily activities are connected to the overall inquiry.)*

Students: What is a good relationship?

J.W.: Right on! Now today we are going to use the setup question: "How do people promote or undermine various kinds of relationships?" *(I put this on the overhead.)* Let's brainstorm what we've already learned or already think about this. *(I am activating their prior knowledge and asking them to bring forward and summarize what we've already learned about the inquiry so it will be available for today's activity.)*

(Students brainstorm, and I record their answers.)

J.W.: Okay, today we are going to learn a questioning scheme, called the "questioning circle" that is really going to help you all be better readers, so let's hear some cheers!

(Students cheer—and boo.)

Pure Questions

J.W.: All right. All right. The reason this is going to help you is because the scheme gets you to ask questions from the three areas of our life we have to combine to really learn and use what we've learned: our own personal experience, our experience of the world including what we've learned in other subjects, and the material we're studying. *(I write these down.)*

J.W.: Now the first type of question is one that is based on your experience, your interests, totally about *you*, but related to the topic. Okay, I'll call this a ME question. It's good to ask this kind first because it frontloads you for reading, making sure you've got some stuff to bring from your life to the reading, which we all have to do whenever we read! *(I remind students of what we have discussed before and try to increase their metacognitive awareness of reading processes.)* Here's mine. *(I write on the board, "Me: What kind of relationships do I pursue and why?")*

J.W.: Does everybody see why this is a good Me question?

Student: It's totally about you.

J.W.: Yes, and as you'll see, this will help me understand Max and the point Mr. Sendak is trying to make through his book! You have to be sure all your questions relate to the inquiry topic you are pursuing. Now I want you to work with your group to come up with one or two Me questions of your own, which we will then share on the overhead.

Students list some of their Me questions on an acetate sheet and share them with the class on the overhead in a technique I call "roundtable." The rest of the class confirms that their questions are Me questions or helps revise them, if necessary. Next I write the other two types of pure questions on the board: "Book: How do Max, his mother, and the Wild Things place themselves inside and outside relationships with others?" and "World: What kinds of groups, teams, and organizations do people want to belong to in the world? What satisfactions do these different groups provide?" We repeat a similar process for each question type. First I explain, model, and then discuss the question type with students, then I ask them to try one or two of their own in groups. They "report out" their questions to the class so we can examine them and confirm or revise them.

Shaded Questions

J.W.: Okay, you querulous questioners, you are rocking and rolling! But now things get a bit more complicated. Now we write "shaded" questions, so-called because you have to combine resources to answer them, like from the text and the world, the text and the self, or the self and the world. These kinds of questions are most excellent because they require us to start combining our personal concerns with the text, or concerns of the subjects we study or the world with the text or ourselves. So this is helping us be good inquirers, because this is what inquirers do!

(I write on the board: "Text and me: How do I treat people who I am happy or upset with? How is this treatment different if I care about them or have to be with them—like in a family or school?")

J.W.: Now, one tip for making your own "text and me question" is to take something important from the text, like an event or idea, and then compare it with how you would deal with that event or idea in your own life.

(I write on the board: "Text and world: How do the relationships in the book compare with the ways society—school, church, the law, sports teams—treats people it approves and disapproves of?")

J.W.: Okay, Reading Rabbits, for this one you need to think about how the topic or major ideas from the book connect to problems or issues or ideas or ways of doing things that we see in different subjects or out in the world. You could even do what I did and say, "How does X from the book compare with Y in the world?" Just a tip. I'll be around to help you. *(I write on the board: "How does X compare to Y?")*

(Next, I write on the board: "World and Me: How do I feel about the way we treat 'outsiders' in our school, town and culture? What other options do I see for treatment of others—e.g. old people who are sent to senior citizen homes—that exist but are not typically practiced in our society/school/town?" I do this one last because kids sometimes find it hard to ask a question that is not anchored to the text. Generally, it's easier if they practice the other two types of shaded questions first.)

J.W.: Ah, this one will be easy for hyperintelligent inquirers like you. All you have to do is think about how you feel or think about a real-world issue that has to do with our inquiry topic. You could start with the stem "How do I feel/think/react to Y, about relationships in the world/relationships I see/etc.?" Just another tip, even though I know you don't need it!

(Kids write questions and report out in roundtables.)

World and me questions

How do I feel...
- When people are mean to each other Just because the look different or have a different intrest?

How should we think...
When people who are really different are close friends?

A student brainstormed World and Me questions for use in a roundtable.

Dense Question:

J.W.: Oh man, we have just about enough time to do this one—woo-hoo! This is the granddaddy of questions: the dense question. And not dense like some middle schoolers but dense because it combines the text with the world and your personal life in one mega-amazing, brain-wrenching question! Here's mine. *(I write on the board: "Inquiry: What can we learn from Max's experience about ways to set ourselves inside and outside of various relationship groups in the world?")*

(Again, I model the question; we discuss how it makes use of the different resources, and then I ask students to create their own questions of this type, which we then review. As we go along, I draw a graphic of how the knowledge resources and the questions we ask of them interrelate.)

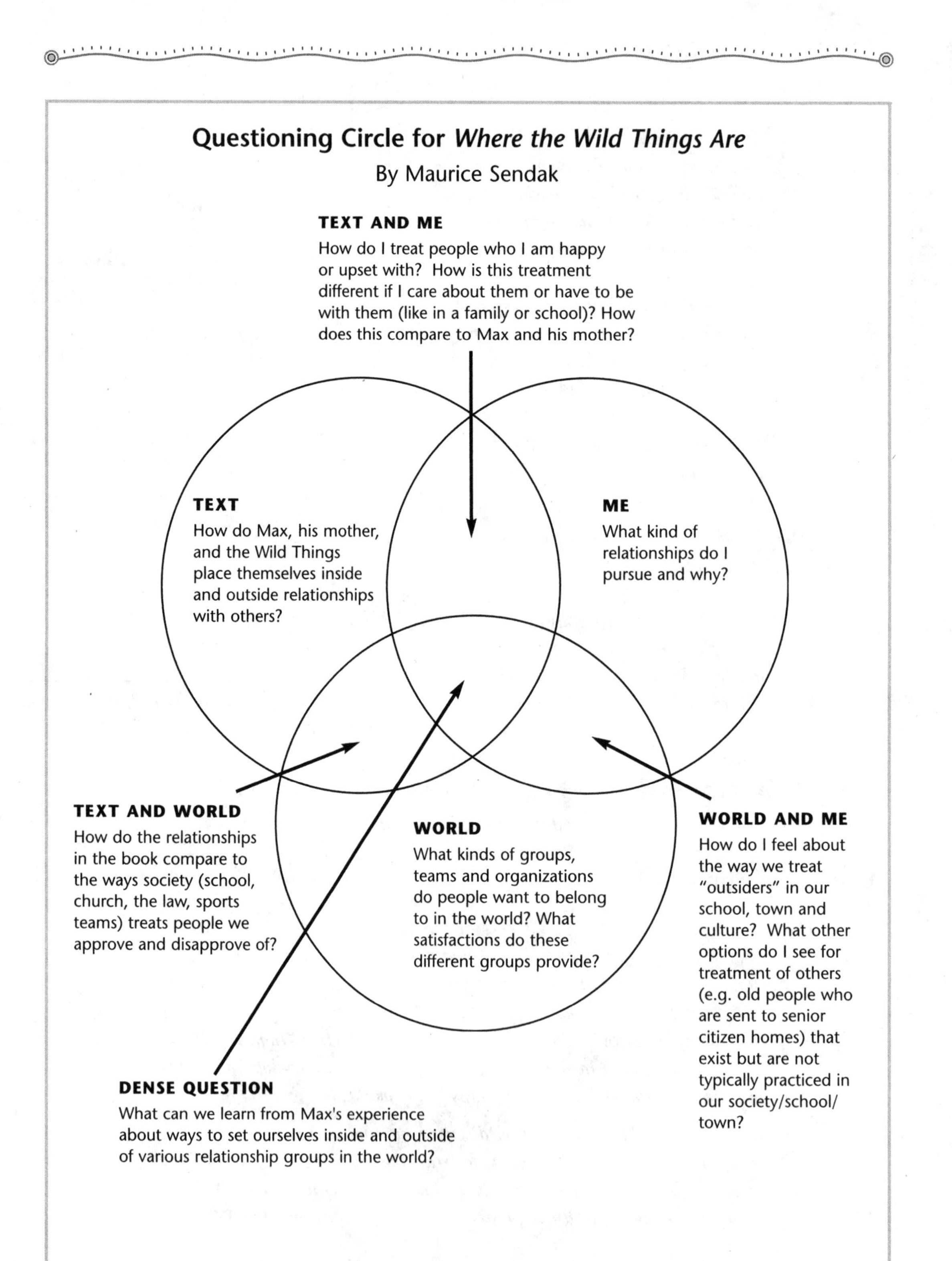

Questioning Circle for *Where the Wild Things Are*
By Maurice Sendak
TEXT AND ME
How do I treat people who I am happy or upset with? How is this treatment different if I care about them or have to be with them (like in a family or school)? How does this compare to Max and his mother?
TEXT
How do Max, his mother, and the Wild Things place themselves inside and outside relationships with others?
ME
What kind of relationships do I pursue and why?
TEXT AND WORLD
How do the relationships in the book compare to the ways society (school, church, the law, sports teams) treats people we approve and disapprove of?
WORLD
What kinds of groups, teams and organizations do people want to belong to in the world? What satisfactions do these different groups provide?
WORLD AND ME
How do I feel about the way we treat "outsiders" in our school, town and culture? What other options do I see for treatment of others (e.g. old people who are sent to senior citizen homes) that exist but are not typically practiced in our society/school/town?
DENSE QUESTION
What can we learn from Max's experience about ways to set ourselves inside and outside of various relationship groups in the world?

J.W.: These are the hardest. In fact, this type of question is always a kind of inquiry question because it makes you see all kinds of connections and ways to apply what you've learned. A tip is to think first about the inquiry topic and then ask what the text says to us and other people about how to use the information or think about the topic, like relationships, when you are out there doing your thing. (Bell rings) You're off the hook for now but we're going to write some of these dense questions later in the week!

Conclusion: Connecting Through Questioning Schemes

Each of these schemes is powerful precisely because it mirrors the trajectory of the inquiry process: Moving students' responses from the factual, through interpretative connection-making, to critical evaluations and applications that are valuable in the world.

Furthermore, these schemes illuminate how the processes of inquiry and design are akin to the processes of expert reading. (See the chart on the next page for more on this.) David Perkins (1996) a cognitive scientist from Harvard University, argues that the metaphor for knowledge is inquiry-based "design"—in other words, knowledge is web-like, interconnected. Knowledge is reusable, extensible and usable. To create knowledge and understanding, students need knowledge of purpose and of how to access, develop, interconnect, structure, and apply data.

All of these questioning schemes help us operate on texts (or on any other data set) as inquirers and knowledge designers, and to extend the meaning we find into our lives and our futures. If our students do not learn to do this kind of work, they will be mired in information, instead of empowered to create and use knowledge. To help our students become inquirers is to help them become more powerful learners and people. We must help them internalize questioning strategies and schemes, help them take on an inquiring mind-set, help them proceed from understanding facts to designing new understandings and critical uses of these understandings. The schemes presented here help students to do just that, and to achieve what fewer than six percent of graduating seniors can do (see NAEPs 2005): identify and explain complex implied relationships, argue for positions and justify conclusions with textual evidence. These skills are necessary not only for true knowledge design and understanding, but for respecting authors and the people they describe, and for democracy itself.

A Comparison of Two Recursive Processes

Inquiry-Based Design	**Reading**
Problem-Definition/issue Identification	Topic Identification/Activate Schema
Ask essential question Decompose task: Ask set-up/subquestions	Set purposes for reading Use global and local questioning
Find existing information get by searching info sources	Decode textual meanings; get by transacting with text
Develop new data—make fuller, bigger, better Fill in niches, create new structures	Make Inferences; elaborate-transact with text seeing local and global patterns of coherence across the text and elaborating
Analyze—examine in detail	Connect text to personal life and world
Organize—to provide a structure to arrange details in to a new whole	Create a structured mental model of the text world
Design—to make a plan, begin to represent what has been learned in a new and usable form	Create new schematic structures by assimilating new learning into existing schematic structures; or by revising existing schema to accommodate the new learning—this can be abetted by using visual tools like SFA, family tree, Venn diagrams, etc.
Present—exhibit and show one's knowledge representations and artifacts; get feedback	Share—discuss, negotiate meanings with other readers; get feedback
Reflect—think seriously upon Consider alternatives	Reflect—consider multiple points of view
Refine and Revise—make the design more polished, elegant, usable	Revise—improve interpretations based on feedback, make more usable and applicable to one's life
Use the knowledge artifact to communicate meanings; solve problems; provide services	Use what has been learned, applying it to thinking, perceiving, behavior
Continue to improve the artifact; provide it to others for their use.	Continue to flesh out interpretations; share and use them in the world.

From Hyperlearning, *Wilhelm and Friedemann, Stenhouse Publishers (1998)*

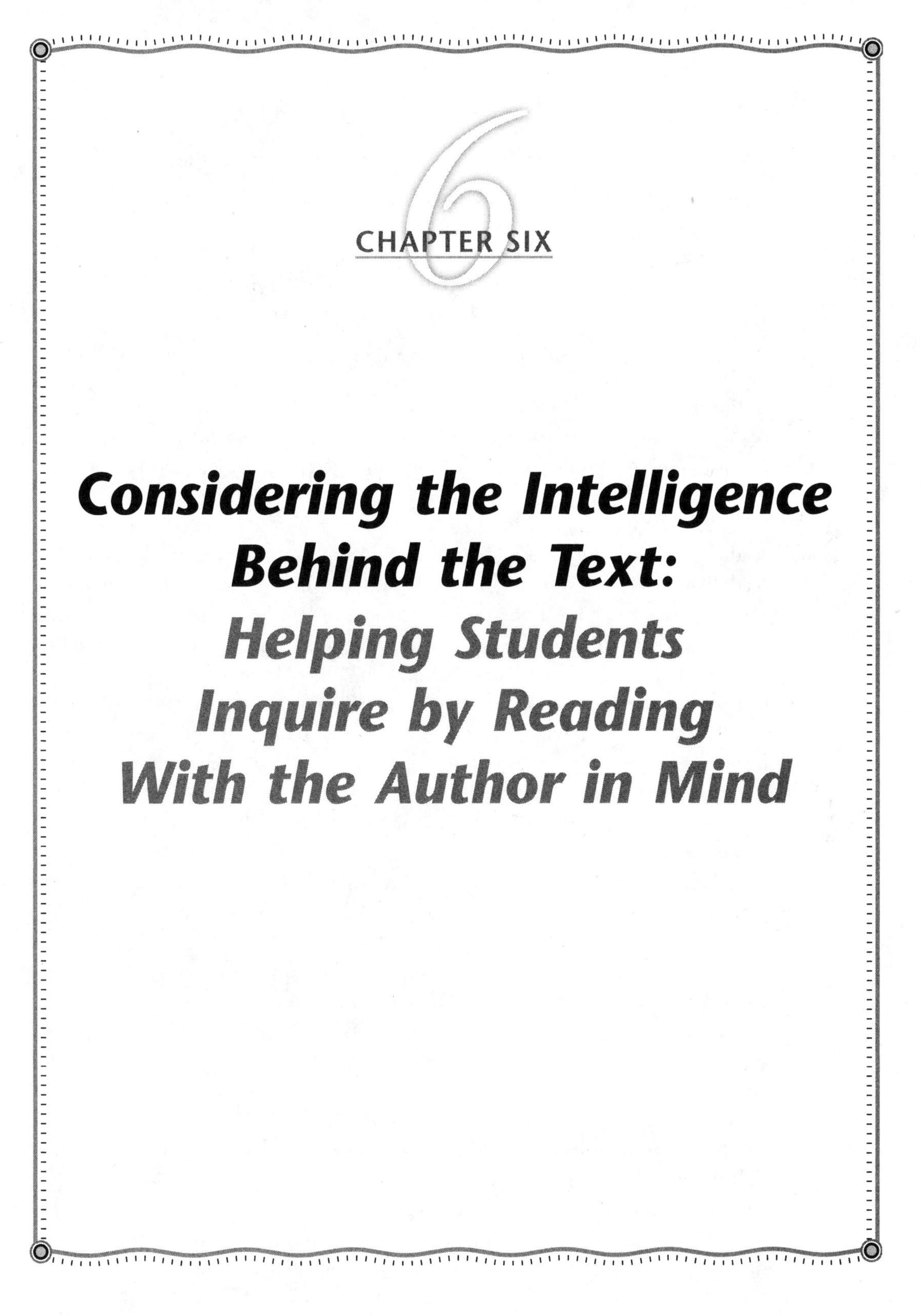

CHAPTER SIX

Considering the Intelligence Behind the Text: Helping Students Inquire by Reading With the Author in Mind

> "What authors would you invite to a dinner party?" seventh grader Cora asked her classmate Joanne.
>
> "It depends what I might want to learn about," Joanne replied, "or how much fun and distraction I might want! Like if I was interested in the Depression I might invite Mildred Taylor and Karen Hesse. But if I wanted to be part of an argument, I'd invite Martin Luther King and Malcolm X!"
>
> "Oh!" Cora exclaimed. "You like theme parties!"

As this dialogue excerpt shows, and as I've found in my various studies of reading, relationships drive much of student reading and learning. In our research on boys' literacy, relationships with teachers were central to student motivation, engagement, and willingness to take risks (Smith and Wilhelm, 2002, 2006). Likewise, relationships with characters were essential to their reading engagement. One student in our studies, Geo, put it this way: "I would read, like, a person's story about slavery and how they got through. Yeah, that sounds pretty good, but I don't want to read about, like, the whole timeline of slavery or the whole timeline of the Holocaust or stuff like that." In my studies leading up to *You Gotta BE the Book* (Wilhelm, 1997), I found that highly engaged readers were also motivated by taking up relationships with authors, and that this deepened their enjoyment and understanding of the issues and meanings that were treated in the text. One student, Cora, said that she was impressed with Sheila Burnaford (author of *The Incredible Journey*) "because she really understands animals!" and that she loved reading Katherine Paterson because she "is a great-hearted person," and that when she reads "her books I feel like I'm getting to know a very kind and sensitive person who has a powerful heart and . . . an ability to understand people."

When we think about the power of relationships in reading and writing, we often miss the idea of relating to an author. Personally, I want my students to know that every text is constructed by someone who is trying to manipulate them into noticing, believing, or doing something. Whether it's Tolstoy's *Anna Karenina*, Stephen J. Gould's *The Mismeasure of Man*, a cartoon, a poem, or an advertisement, a powerful mind and complex heart are behind the composition, hoping to convince you of something.

I want students to respect the intelligence behind the text, and to converse with the meanings constructed by that author by reading the text in the way it was constructed to be read. I then want students to ask themselves how they feel about the meaning they were asked to construct and decide for themselves if they want to accept, reject, or in some way adapt the textual meaning.

Authorial Reading: A Way of Seeing and Responding to a Text's Architecture of Ideas

Rabinowitz and Smith (1998) have coined the concept "authorial reading" as a way to think about conversing with authors. Aligned with transactional reader-response theory, authorial reading theory posits that readers must respond to something particular: namely, the deep meaning that an author has constructed through the medium of text. Readers must first understand what the author meant to convey, and then they need to evaluate the meaning and transform it to be of use in their own situation and life projects.

To read authorially is to read a text respectfully, the way an author crafted it to be read. This is a skill that is near and dear to my heart, since I believe it is essential to inquiry, learning from others, and democracy itself. When we teach authorial reading, a student learns how to read the meanings of an author by knowing how these meanings were constructed and "coded" into the text. By coded, I mean the myriad conventions that authors employ, from the poet's use of symbolism, white space and assonance to the red herrings and character clues implanted by mystery writers, to the core assumption of all writers that a reader will bring certain background knowledge to bear on the text. Here is another way to think about it: As readers, we expect a writer to bring certain things to the text in order to meet our satisfaction. But way before we open the book covers, the author *has set expectations of us*, his audience. With authorial reading, we meet an author's expectations. And then some.

In his wonderful book on the ethics of reading, *The Company We Keep* (1983), Wayne Booth proclaims that we can and do learn from texts and one another, but only if we learn how to listen carefully and respectfully, working hard to understand the other in his or her own terms before judging and using what we learn. Authorial reading, and questioning schemes that promote it, helps students pay respectful attention and then contend with, accept, adapt or resist and, finally, make new meanings and applications.

Authorial Reading and Inquiry: Complementary Pursuits

Authorial reading is entirely consistent with the concept of inquiry. In each pursuit, our job is to first understand what is already thought and known. But if we stop here, as schools usually do, then we are merely information consumers instead of *producers of knowledge* who have learned and practiced how to create, evaluate, and use new understandings. Unless we help our students go beyond comprehension, they will not learn how to participate in communities of practice as developing mathematicians, historians, scientists, ethicists, linguists, and the like. We have to help them see that comprehension of an author's articulated message is the beginning, not the end, of knowledge construction and use.

Learning depends at first on topical research, studying and interpretation of what is already known, but critical inquiry and authorial reading requires us to evaluate and to move beyond our interpretations. It asks us to apply our new understandings. In critical inquiry we imagine a more complex reality beyond the limited perspective and the limited description offered by our own experience or a particular text. We consider what part of a new perspective we may want to embrace, consider more deeply, adapt and transform, or even resist. We reflect on what the text or materials under discussion—and our critical response to it— should mean to us in individual and social ways.

Authorial reading resonates with Bakhtin's (1986) concept of "reciprocity." As Nystrand (1997) puts it: acts we might consider to be "individual," like mailing a letter, reading, or any kind of learning, are in fact social, since "each is premised on appropriate and respective acts by reciprocal others. For example, mailing a letter assumes postal workers and the letter's recipient and assumes particular expectations of these parties; writers likewise assume a reader who will know how to read their text, etc."

Reading, in these terms, is the evolution of understanding through the co-construction of meaning that occurs in "the unique interaction between author and reader, the play of two consciousnesses" (Bakhtin & Medvedev, 1986, p. 128; cited in Nystrand, 1997).

Vygotskians call this kind of interplay the achievement of "intersubjectivity" in which we take on the understandings of another and make this understanding our own, however tentatively. In effect, we try on other perspectives and ways of knowing before taking them on, appropriating or adapting them in some form for ourselves.

In authorial reading, we make the attempt to be the reader the author imagined when constructing the text, attempting to understand the text the way it was coded to be understood. In so doing, we work toward achieving reciprocity or intersubjectivity with the "intelligence behind the text."

Let's use the example of conversation as an analogy. If we are talking about an important issue, and I interrupt you and say "This is what you should really be thinking . . ." or "A truly informed view of this issue would be . . ." you would think to yourself, and rightly so: this guy is a jerk. He didn't even pay me the consideration to try and figure out what I was trying to say.

But if I listen carefully and work very hard to understand you, asking clarifying questions and rephrasing your ideas, conversing with you about your thinking, and checking to see if I fully understood, you would feel respected and attended to. Even if at the end I said, "I must respectfully disagree" or "Though I respect your position, I would amend it for myself in this way" or "Have you ever considered . . ." you would still feel we had a meaningful and useful conversation.

This is the point of authorial reading, to respect the author and her text, and after comprehending it, to grant it the seriousness of reflection and evaluation so we make what we learn from that conversation our own. In this way, authorial reading is learning centered. I tell my students that "everyone here is a teacher and a student. We have 30 teachers and 30 students in this room. All of you and myself. And every author we read is our teacher. We don't have to accept what we learn from every teacher, but we must hear and attend to them."

I have adapted two questioning schemes in ways that are very useful for promoting this kind of democratic dialogue with texts: Questioning the Author and Hillocks' (1980) questioning hierarchy. Both work not only for authorial reading, but for inquiry, as both schemes mirror the trajectory of the inquiry process that moves from topical research and understanding to critical inquiry and application of deep thematic meanings. Both schemes help students attend to how meaning is constructed and communicated, and thus to read like a writer, and, conversely, write like a reader.

Questioning the Author (QtA)

The first approach we'll look at is Questioning the Author (Beck, McKeown et al., 1997; Beck & McKeown, 2006). Its premise is that when we support our students' comprehension *during* reading, we are intervening at the optimum point in the reading process. And when we help students realize that any text is "someone's thoughts written down," it gives them the confidence to wrestle with a text's ideas and construct meaning. In becoming aware that an author is fallible, students, especially those who struggle with reading, feel more confident about their ability to comprehend. They go into reading with the attitude: Maybe sometimes it's not *their* fault that they didn't get a particular part—maybe the author wasn't clear.

Beck and McKeown use two question types as the key instructional tools in QtA discussions: the Initiating Query and the Follow-Up Query. (They use the word *query* to distinguish these moves from traditional questions, which often only root out literal recall.) These queries are developed by the teacher before a lesson and posed as students read a text *for the first time*. The queries prompt students to engage with one another about the text and consider what the author is attempting to communicate. Over time, students internalize this active, questioning stance to become stronger readers—capable of authorial reading.

Though a simple scheme, it works powerfully to promote deeper thinking and discussion, and to extend students' interpretations. As an overview of how Beck and McKeown conceive of it, here is an excerpt from their book, *Improving Comprehension with Questioning the Author* (2006).

Helping Students Take Notice of the Text: Some Sample Queries

Queries tend to be open-ended. They place the responsibility for building meaning on the students. A query's goal is more important than the way it is worded. The major goals of Initiating Queries are to make public the messages or ideas presented by the author. They draw attention to key text ideas and remind students that those ideas were written by an author.

Initiating Queries: Opening Up Discussion

What is the author trying to say here?
What do you think the author wants us to know?
What is the author talking about?
What's the important message in this section?

Follow-Up Queries: Guiding Students to Connect Ideas

Follow-Up Queries help focus the content and direction of a discussion and assist students in integrating and connecting ideas to build meaning. Now let's consider examples of Follow-Up Queries.

To encourage kids to consider the ideas behind the author's words . . .

So what does the author mean right here?
That's what the author said, but what did the author mean?

To help students relate information from different parts of the text and see that a connection or linking piece of information may be missing from the text . . .

Does that make sense with what the author told us before?
How does that fit in with what the author told us?

Adapted from *Improving Comprehension with Questioning the Author* by Isabel L. Beck and Margaret G. McKeown (Scholastic, 2006)

To plan a QtA lesson, teachers first select a text and then look for a text's hot spots—important moments that either house key information or that may be tricky for students in some way. This is called "segmenting" the text (dividing it up into short sections to be followed by QtA discussion). The teacher develops queries for each of these portions so she will have a blueprint to guide students as they hit these crucial junctures in their reading. Next, the teacher then reads the text aloud as students follow along. After each segment is read, the teacher poses queries for discussion (or has students choose queries from a menu).

In my experience, as students become familiar with QtA, it works well for teachers to pose queries to students during a read-aloud or think-aloud (Wilhelm, 2001) or ask students to do the same, whether using QtA in small or large groups. The queries should prompt students to converse with and challenge the author and see various connections between details, or between text, self, and the world. For instance, if students are studying geography, instead of asking, *What are nomads?* or *Why did people become nomads?* teachers frame queries such as *How does that information about nomads fit in with what the author is telling us about the geography and climate of the Sahara and what it takes to survive there?* or *What kind of nomadic things do we do to survive or improve our lives and how is this similar and different from the Saharan nomads?* (Beck & McKeown, 2002).

Using QtA to Promote Authorial Reading of Texts

In my middle-school unit on *What is community and where do I fit in?* we read the novel *Bud, Not Buddy* (Curtis, 1999). The novel takes place in Michigan during the Depression, and involves the orphan Bud and his search for his father. My students had been using QtA throughout the unit, so they were able to use it on their own as they began to read this text. In this case, using it on their own meant that groups of four to five students read and discussed the novel together; my role was to get them started and check in every now and then.

First, I had them read the jacket copy, the author bio, and consider the title of the book. Then, I asked them to read the first chapter at home that night. The next day, I prompted them to begin their discussion with the following queries, which I put on the overhead. They were then free to use any other queries from their menu sheets (see page 140).

Initiating Queries:

Who is the author of this novel? What do we know about this author?

What is the author writing about? What is the general subject or topic?

Follow-Up Queries:

What are the most important details so far? Why do you think so?

What does the author want the reader to notice in this segment? And think, believe, or do as a result?

Why is the author telling us this information right now? In this way? In this order?

What ideas are puzzling? What would we like to know more about?

Here's a transcript from one group's discussion after reading Chapter 1. I've bolded their use of queries:

Jason: Okay. Down to business. What I want to know first is, **Who is the author?**

Dashiel: It says on the back that he wrote *The Watsons Go to Birmingham* and that he is from Flint, Michigan.

Rebecca: Hey, this story is set in Michigan, and the picture of Herman was from Flint.

Jason: Yeah?

Roderick: So, I'm just saying maybe the author is writing about what he is knowing from being from Michigan, or whatever.

Sam: You know what the teacher says, "Write what you know about."

Dashiel: **What's he writing about—the topic, I mean?**

Sam: Well, fitting in, obviously, since that's our inquiry. Bud doesn't fit in at the home, and he hasn't fit in his foster homes, and he probably won't fit in this next one.

Jason: But he thinks that if he finds his dad that he'll fit in. He'll be where he belongs.

Sam: I don't think Herman is his dad. No way.

Jason: Why not?

Sam: It's a whaddayacallit. A trick. We're supposed to believe that's his dad but it's not.

Dashiel: What makes you so sure?

Sam: It would be too easy. **The author is going to tell us that fitting in is way more complicated than finding your dad.** He'll fit in somewhere, but it'll be blood and guts until the end of the book.

Jason: Oh, just ruin the whole story for us! (*They laugh.*)

Dashiel: He could still make that point and Herman could still be his dad.

Sam: We'll see, brother. We'll see.

Jason: Mmm, mmm, mmm. I think Herman is his dad but he's not so nice.

Roderick: Yeah, for some reason Bud is on his own. If Herman is his dad, then he is not on the case.

Sam: Nice catch, Roderick! (*They give each other fist fives.*)

Roderick: Okay, my turn, I guess. **What are the most important details so far?**

Dashiel: He's an orphan.

Sam: He's in a home.

Dashiel: He's going to a new home. He got beat in his other foster homes.

Jason: His mom died and he doesn't know much about his family. Just has that picture and stuff.

Sam: Okay, here's mine: **What's puzzling?**

Dashiel: Why is the author going on about Jerry?

Jason: Yeah, why is that, since Jerry is going to be going his own way, which is out of the story?

Sam: **I think it gives the author a chance to talk about Bud's past and show how he's a good guy and all the trouble he's had. It sets up all the problems.**

What to Notice

Notice how the boys immediately get to work, aided by the query guide I provided. Even though they don't spend too much time on any one query, they stay on task. As soon as a few turns have been taken around a query, someone steps in with a new one. Every boy responds and every boy poses his own query from the list.

Notice, too, how the boys focus on the author who composed this text, as well as how and why he has composed it the way he did to communicate meaning.

These seventh graders, aided by the QtA queries, are already practicing a sophisticated authorial reading that many older readers never achieve.

A Menu of Queries

Following is a menu of queries that promote authorial reading that I've found useful with my own students. I might list several of these queries on the overhead or chalkboard to help students query a text and one another as they read. I might also provide menus of queries to students for their use during discussion.

Initiating Queries for Use Early in a Text Reading

(You can call them "start off queries," if your students find this an easier term.)

- Who is the author?
- Who is the intended audience for this piece? (Am I part of this audience? What would I have to know, believe, or be to become part of this audience?)
- What does the author want her audience to know, believe, or do? Why?
- What special reading strategies is the author asking me to use?
- What is the author writing about? (What is the general subject or topic?)
- What important information has the author presented so far? (What are the key details?)
- What might be her purpose and agenda in writing this text?
- What point of view or group perspective is being expressed?
- What is the author's point so far? (What is the main idea or central focus? What conclusion do the key details add up to? What does the author want me to know, think, believe, or do?)

Follow-Up Queries for Use While Students Are Immersed in a Text

(My students and I also call them "local-level queries.")

- What does the author want the reader to notice in this segment—and think, believe, or do as a result?
- Why is the author telling us this information right now? In this way? In this order?
- How is the text organized to reinforce key details and the main point the author is trying to make?
- Did the author explain this clearly? Are we convinced of her point of view?

- Is this consistent with what we knew before reading? With what the author communicated earlier in the reading?
- What differences or similarities do we see between ideas from the reading, and between these ideas and those from other readings and from our experience/the world?
- What ideas are puzzling? What would we like to know more about?
- What strategies do we need to use to read this part of the text? How do we know? (What tip-offs for strategy use have been coded into the text?)
- Why did certain things happen? What might have caused these events?
- How would you act or feel if you were a character or person featured in this text?
- How might or should what we are learning influence the future? Our personal behavior? World consequences? What might be the future effects of the situations described?
- What could be done to change or improve this situation, or similar ones in the world?
- How do the ideas connect to what we already care about? How do they relate to our own values, attitudes, or beliefs?
- What is the author's point so far? (What is the main idea or central focus? What conclusion do the key details add up to? What does the author want us to know, think, believe, or do?)
- How well does the author convince us to think or behave in a certain way? Is this case made explicitly or implicitly?

Hillocks' Questioning Hierarchy

My all-time favorite questioning scheme is George Hillocks' questioning hierarchy (1980). He calls it a hierarchy for understanding literature, but I have found it useful for helping students understand most any carefully constructed text, whether it's narrative fiction, poetry, or expository nonfiction.

The hierarchy consists of a carefully constructed set of question types based on the assertion that "before students can deal with abstractions . . . they must be able to deal with the literal and inferential content of the work" (p. 306).

The Hillocks hierarchy uses seven levels of questions to move students from the literal to the inferential—and then to two kinds of abstractions: authorial generalizations (themes about the world expressed in the work) and structural generalizations (how the text was constructed to express these ideas). The hierarchy fosters a level of understanding about how texts are constructed that no other scheme does. You can also see, in the exploration that follows, how it encompasses and then goes beyond the different kinds of reading activity required by QARs and the different resources that must be brought to bear when using the circle.

Hillocks slices questions types more finely than the QAR scheme does, to show that there are different kinds of factual (right there) questions and inferential (think and search) questions that are dependent on each other. Factual questions are divided into three types: questions that ask for the basic stated information, those that ask for key details, and those that ask for stated relationships. Inferential questions are divided into two types: those looking for simple implied relationships and those looking for complex implied relationships.

Then Hillocks takes a unique turn to consider thematic meanings and how they are expressed through the codes and structures of the text. Authorial generalizations apply to the world and inform personal action; structural generalizations help students consider transferable ways of reading and writing on their own. In this way, the hierarchy also considers the resources and ends of reading highlighted by the questioning circle.

Hierarchy questions are asked after reading, since students need to have a sense of textual coherence and how various details relate to one another.

Using the Hierarchy to Assess Student Understanding

One of the most powerful features of the Hillocks hierarchy is its heuristic value for teachers as they assess student comprehension. This is the only questioning hierarchy that has ever been demonstrated through research studies to actually work as a hierarchy, i.e., answering a level-one question is a prerequisite to answering a level-two question and so forth. That means teachers can use it to assess exactly where a particular student experiences difficulties with a particular text. For example, in my own classroom research using the hierarchy, I've found that my middle schoolers typically have trouble with complex implied relationships, and some with simple implied relationships. My high school students typically break down with complex implied relationships and the generalization questions. Knowing this helps me plan my instruction. I pitch questions, strategies, and activities around helping students make inferences and generalizations, and I can adapt instruction for groups of students who struggle with similar question types. It also assists me because I know not to ask students to identify authorial generalizations unless they can successfully negotiate the prerequisite simple implied and complex implied relationship questions.

For example, when we read *Romeo and Juliet*, I begin each class with a short gut check by asking my students two or three questions from the previous reading. By asking questions of different types, I can determine at what point comprehension is breaking down, and where I need to focus attention. Below are some sample questions that help students build the prerequisite understanding for addressing authorial generalizations—the ability to take major points away from the reading so they can be used and critiqued.

Level 1: Basic Stated Information

After Act I, I ask:

Who are the two main characters in the play?
Who are the two families whose experiences are explored in the play?

This question type establishes whether students can identify and comprehend literal information repeated throughout the text that forms the foundation of understanding. If any student misses this, I know that he or she was "out to lunch" and really needs to be helped.

Level 2: Key Details

Who puts on the party where Romeo and Juliet meet?

This question type determines if a student comprehends a detail that is crucial to understanding the reading but is only stated in one place. If any of my students missed this detail from Act I, then I need to reinforce it, since it informs what follows—Tybalt's anger, the ensuing fight with Mercutio, etc.

Level 3: Stated Relationships

As we proceed into Act II, basic stated information and key details build up and create the kind of patterns and relationships that are essential to understanding a rich story. So I begin to ask various relationship questions, starting with the stated relationship question.

What is the relationship between the Capulets and Montagues?
What does Juliet's family say about Romeo?
What does the nurse tell Juliet to do about Romeo?

This question type ascertains whether a student can identify an explicitly stated relationship between two characters, groups, events, issues, or other pieces of information. The relationship is often causal and should have an effect on the action and meaning of the story. Students who do not notice and comprehend stated relationships will be unable to proceed to the inferential level of reading. Students who cannot answer this question type need help to do so.

Literature's unique power derives from the fact that it does not tell you what it means. You have to figure it out—and that inferential work is where all the challenge, joy, surprise, and emotional edge of literature resides. Literature requires that we make our own connections and make our own meanings in conversation with it. Inferring and generalizing are essential elements of reading literature, and the ability to answer the three kinds of literal questions listed above (about basic stated information, key details, and stated relationships) are the prerequisites.

Level 4: Simple Implied Relationships

Moving through the play, I provide gut-check questions such as these:

Why does Mercutio hate Tybalt?

Why does Friar Laurence agree to help Romeo and Juliet?

Why does the Nurse agree to help Juliet?

Why does Juliet's father become so angry about Juliet's reticence to marry Paris?

This question type determines whether a reader has recognized an implied, unstated relationship between a few key details that usually appear close to one another in the text. This kind of question ups the ante, since it asks students to move beyond literal decoding to seeing unstated connections and the meaning of those connections. Now the reader is truly engaging in making inferences. If a student fails to see the implied connections here, then I may need to do some thinking aloud, drama/action strategy work, small-group work—some activity that puts them in the characters' places, and in the world of the story, so that they can bring their own life experiences to bear on their understanding of characters' reactions and feelings.

Level 5: Complex Implied Relationships

This is where the reading rubber hits the road. This is where almost all of my middle school and high school students need some help. I begin to ask these questions as we enter the final phase of reading in Acts IV and V.

How does the relationship between Romeo and Juliet evolve throughout the play?

How does the relationship of Juliet and her parents develop through the play? The relationship between Friar Laurence and Romeo/Romeo and his friends?

Why do the relationships develop in these ways?

There seem to be many reasons, situations, people, forces, that encourage Romeo and Juliet to fall deeply in love. Cite three of these and explain which one you think is the most important, or explain how different reasons are related.

> "What made his intellect so admirable was his ability to connect seemingly separate developments and truths in one field to development in another: he could connect dots where few of his colleagues could even see the dots, let alone relate them."
>
> — David Halberstam, on Stephen Jay Gould's ability to see complex, implied relationships

These questions reveal whether a student can infer relationships between a large number of details that are spread across the text. The student must therefore be able to "identify the necessary details, discern whatever patterns exist among them, and then draw the appropriate inference" (Hillocks, 1980, p. 308).

I may give students a day or two to consider this kind of question before asking for an answer. It is best to have students consider these questions in groups. When they give their answers, they should be able to explain how they came up with them and justify them with details from the text, the world, and their own personal experiences. (The 2003 and 2005 NAEPs show that fewer than 6 percent of graduating high school seniors are adept at seeing and justifying complex implied relationships and authorial generalizations; this is because they are rarely given assistance. Without these skills, students cannot think about or use what they read—certainly a problem in a democratic society.)

Items in the Pocket Activity/Tea Parties

One way to introduce complex implied relationships is with an activity called *items in the pocket.* The teacher makes a list of what was found in a character's pocket. As each item is read (the teacher could also produce the actual items), the students make inferences about the character. By connecting new details to the previous ones, they see how a web of meaning is created through the patterns expressed by the accumulated items.

For example, you could tell students that a character's pockets contained keys, coins, and a wallet. Such a list doesn't reveal much about the character, but it can kick off a discussion about what kinds of details are most salient for constructing character. You could then reveal that the keys are connected to the belt with a chain, that some of the coins are Canadian, and that the wallet contains lists of phone numbers, including several women and an entry for "grandmother." Other items can be added, like an ironed Hermès linen hankie from Paris, or gobs of lint and used candy wrappers. Students see how each succeeding detail must be added to the previous ones to create a pattern that reveals a fuller picture of the character.

As another way to assist students at this level, I've adapted the idea of a tea party (see Wilhelm, 2003). I make a few sets of excerpts, with quotes focusing on different characters, ideas, or themes. (You can use one text, or excerpts from several.) I hand out a single excerpt to each student. Students then wander around the classroom, sharing their quotes. They group themselves with other students who have quotes that are part of the same pattern, that make the same point, or that are about the same character or topic. They then work together to identify all the connections between their quotes and report out to the class. I usually put all the quotes that I think go together on an overhead so that when groups report out, the other class members can read them and see if they agree with the patterns of connection the reporting group saw.

Having students complete cluster webs of key events or details can also help them see complex implied relationships.

Level 6: Authorial Generalization

This type of question is crucial, since it gets at the meaning we are to take away from our reading. Teachers and textbooks almost always ask such questions without first having the students do the prerequisite work with simple and complex implied relationships. These questions should be asked at the end of a reading, since the conclusion is typically crucial to the author's thematic meaning. At the end of Act V, I ask:

> **What is Shakespeare communicating about the forces that disrupt relationships?**

If students are novices at answering this type of question, it's a good idea to formulate a question that cues them in some way toward the answer.

What does the fate of Romeo and Juliet and the direct causes leading to this fate communicate about the threats to healthy relationships?

Once students are more sophisticated, though, it is important to be careful not to cue them.

Questions of this type build on Level 5 to determine what students believe the text implies about the world beyond the text or about the human condition. They are about what is often called the *theme, point, main idea,* or *central focus* of a text. This is not to be confused with a topic statement, such as "the play is about relationships." In contrast, such questions address the larger world. Notice that answering a question of this type depends on understanding various relationships of details throughout the text. It demands a sophisticated and detailed response in which students must consider "the proposition(s) that the story might be said to represent" (Hillocks, 1980, p. 308). Students must be capable of justifying the generalization with the trajectory of how details work together throughout the text to express a particular and conclusive point. They must also consider the ending and how situations have changed due to various factors.

This is a complicated business, and if students have trouble, I often use the simplified version of the hierarchy (see page 148). If I used opinionaires or surveys as front-loading techniques, I can help students by referring them to the themes discussed there. I might ask them what statements in the opinionaire the author would most agree or disagree with and ask them to justify their responses (see opinionaire on p. 71).

Level 7: Structural Generalization

This kind of question cannot be asked until the students have read the text and articulated and justified an authorial generalization. At this level they are reflecting on how the text was structured to make the particular point expressed in the authorial generalization. They are now "reading like a writer." At this point, they can reflect upon the total structure of the text and how it guided their participatory meaning-making as they read.

Here's the one I used:

How does Shakespeare use references to passion (or family or religion) throughout the play to develop a major theme about relationships?

As Hillocks (1980) puts it: "Questions in this category require the reader to explain how parts of the work operate together to achieve certain effects" (p. 308).

Simplified Hierarchy Adaptation: The Questioning Ladder

The Hillocks hierarchy has clear and powerful uses for middle and high school readers. But I would hasten to say that this technique can be equally powerful for younger students. In fact, all of the techniques and schemes in this book can be adapted for use with various groups and levels.

National demonstration-site participant Kelli Olson adapted Hillocks's hierarchy for use with her students in grades 3 to 4. She calls the hierarchy "the Questioning Ladder" and renames the question types in third-and-fourth-grade-friendly language. She has students proceed up the ladder "step by step." Kelli's "ladder" (on page 149) is based on a study of the book *Frindle*, by Andrew Clements. They come from a unit on *How do I balance my needs and rights with those of others?*

Kelli opted not to focus on structural generalizations. I applaud her for making her own call. As with any questioning scheme, you need to choose what your students need and how your use of the scheme will help them meet their needs. Remember, you are the greatest authority on your students' learning in your classroom. You should adapt techniques in ways that make sense to assist your students' learning. Kelli, for example, had her students create question cubes after they read texts, with a different question type on each face of the cube. They then played a questioning game in which they rolled the cubes like dice to determine which question they would ask their peers.

Like the other types of questioning schemes, the hierarchy mirrors the inquiry process: inquirers must first understand established meanings and must then perceive patterns and interpret the meanings of various connections. Finally, they must understand the point expressed by the structure of the data, and how to use this meaning to think and do things in the world. For these reasons, the hierarchy is a powerful scheme for helping students inquire deeply into how authors create meaning, and to achieve the deep understanding of the authorial reader. Once students understand a text on the author's terms, they are free to dispute the expressed meaning, resist or transform it in some way. This is the kind of conversation that brings into play both respect and resistance, and that is so vital to democratic thinking and living.

Questioning Ladder for *Frindle*

Just the Facts!
Questions to Help Us Establish the Facts

Step 1: Obvious Information

Create a question about a detail that is repeated and can be found right there in the book.

Example: What is Nick Allen known for at his school?

Step 2: Key Detail

Create a question about a detail that is very important to the story's plot and helps move this plot forward.

Example: What is Mrs. Granger's passion in teaching?

Step 3: Explained Relationships/"How Come?"

Create a question that focuses attention on a direct statement about how two events or details are related. This question might explain why or "how come" something happened between two things, but the answer must be directly stated.

Example: "How come" Nick challenges Mrs. Granger?

But What Does It Mean?
Questions to help us figure things out

Step 4: Connect Some Dots/Playing Detective

Create a question about two or three clues that are close together and work together in some way. The question should require the answerer to "connect the dots" to determine a solution or meaning that is not stated in the text.

Example: In what different ways does Mrs. Granger popularize the word *frindle*?

Step 5: Connecting Lots of Dots/Playing Super Detective

Create a question where a person has to use many details from throughout the whole text to arrive at a solution that isn't right in the book.

Example: What are the three biggest reasons why Nick chooses to continue his "battle" with Mrs. Granger? How are they related? Which do you think is most important?

Step 6: Walking in the Author's Shoes

Create a question that asks about one of the Big Ideas the author expresses in the story. This should be an idea we can apply to our lives and the world beyond the story.

Example: What is the author saying about challenging authority? What would he say are some of the positive and negative effects of challenging authority?

—Kelli Olson

Information Versus Knowledge and Understanding

from Wilhelm, Jeffrey D. (2004) *Reading Is Seeing.* NY: Scholastic

Information	Knowledge and Understanding
is received from outside sources	is socially and culturally constructed; must involve personal effort, contributions, and connection-making to be internalized by an individual
may not involve a mental model	involves creating a new mental model (to the learner) for understanding a concept, process, or genre
is usually decontextualized; taught separately from use	is always contextualized—learned and applied in a situation in which the knowledge is required and used
is recapitulated	is transformed, transmediated, re-represented in new ways new strategies are learned through interaction with the data
is submitted or sometimes displayed (e.g., homework)	is usable over time by self and others; can be adapted and transferred to new situations
is "schoolish"—only counts in school contexts	is "toolish"—can help to perform tasks and extend human abilities in the world outside of school
is completed and then discarded (e.g., term papers, tests)	is archival and extensible over time, by creator and others; can be continually revised and built upon
is fragmented	is structured and systematic—there is a clear relationship and interplay between structure, details, and use
is linear.	is weblike—data is interconnected within and across sources, like Internet hotlinks
is established, inert, static	is generative, additive, dynamic, evolving, revisable
is accepted, unjustified	is justified—reasoning is made visible and accountable—and reservations are acknowledged and responded to
is considered to be "factual."	is considered to be socially constructed and therefore revisable, extensible, and so on.
is the end of learning.	Finding information is the beginning of learning.
Teaching is the donation of information to learners.	Teaching is assisting learners in learning and problem-solving performances with data and strategies for the end of constructing deep understandings.
Knowing involves the what; memorization and recapitulation of information.	Knowing involves the why, how and what, in that order of priority. Human purposes for the knowledge is foregrounded.
The purpose of learning is telling back.	Learning is the application of knowledge, which continues to develop and evolve throughout life as it is applied to new situations.

Authorial reading positions students as meaning-makers and requires knowledge design and understanding on their part. Receiving information, like literal comprehension, does not.

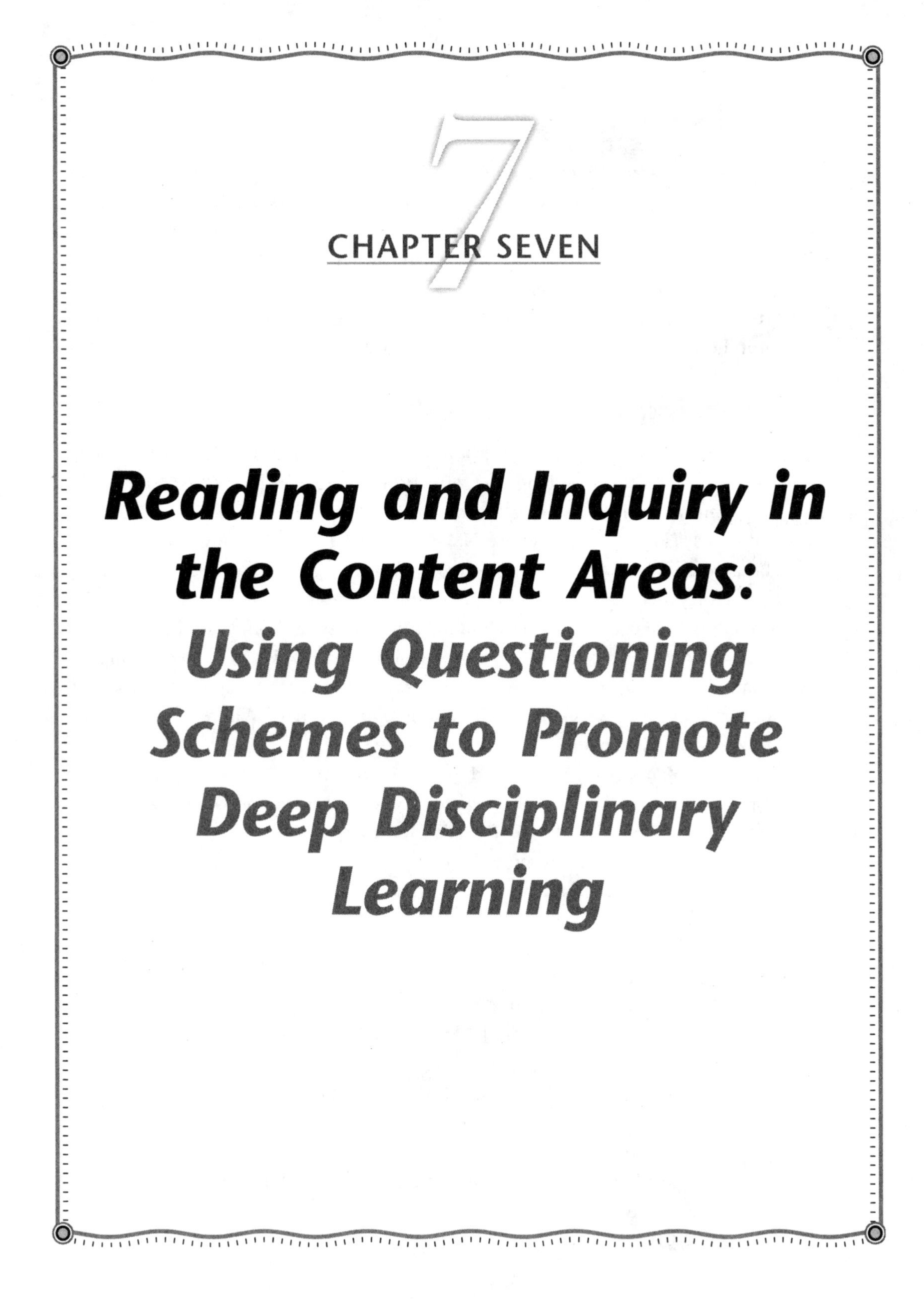

7

CHAPTER SEVEN

Reading and Inquiry in the Content Areas: Using Questioning Schemes to Promote Deep Disciplinary Learning

In this chapter I'll explore how the general questions presented in Chapter 4 and the questioning schemes presented in Chapters 5 and 6 can be used to organize content-area inquiry. We'll see how this can be done in ways that will help students become "developing experts" who participate in the critical inquiry of math, science, social studies, or another field. And they will do so with great gusto because they will be doing the work of the discipline—not the freeze-dried busy work they're so often faced with in school.

Learning to Speak "Ag"

When my daughters Fiona and Jasmine were younger, our family friend Bruce Hunter taught them Ag language, affectionately referred to as "Ag." To speak it, you simply put the syllable *ag* in front of all vowels. So, "Hello, Bruce Hunter" becomes "Hag-ell-ag-o, Brag-uce Hag-unt-ag-er!" In no time, my daughters became fluent. In fact, they can speak it and understand it at amazing speeds.

Fiona recently got in trouble at school for designating on official school paperwork that Ag is a foreign language she speaks at home. It took me some time to convince the school testing coordinator that this was *not* a real language (particularly since the school qualifies for extra funding based on the number of nonnative English speakers who attend). I asked her, "Where do you think this language is spoken? Ag-afastan?"

Anyway, my girls recently had some friends over to our house. As they often do, they spoke in Ag when they wanted to say something private to each other.

"What are you speaking?" Fiona's friend Katie asked.

"Ag language," Fiona replied.

"I thought your family was from Switzerland," Katie replied.

"We are."

"Do they speak Ag in Switzerland?"

"No," Fiona replied.

"I'm *so* confused!" squealed Katie.

"I thought you said you spoke Math language," Julia commented.

The girls all laughed.

I entered the conversation at this point: "There are lots of people who do speak Math language. You should be learning to speak and think in Math language at school."

"Who would want to speak Math?" Katie asked with a grimace.

"Or Science?" Julia added.

Of course, it was all in fun, but the conversation was troubling to me: the girls had no interest in learning to speak the language of mathematicians or scientists, and they went on to talk about how much they disliked their math and science classes.

I remember feeling the same way in school. Only as an adult have I discovered something of the wonder, fun, and power of thinking, and speaking like a mathematician or a scientist. Now I was hearing—and not for the first time—that my daughters and their friends were typecasting these fields of study as dullsville. What goes awry in our teaching of such subjects, generation after generation?

Issues of Engagement and Competence

Several national commissions have identified students' motivation as a foremost challenge teachers face today. It therefore behooves us to understand the relationship between students' interest and engagement and their disciplinary competence. Traditional information-driven approaches zap the energy of teaching and learning, and undermine the capacity of students to apply what they learn to their lives in ways that will continue to increase their competence. As one colleague of mine maintains, "Kids don't become readers because they are hooked on the *cr* blend." Kids get hooked by developing real competence that can accomplish real goals. They get hooked by being apprenticed into a real community of practice. They want to be insiders, members of the club. We must hook them and move them along a *continuum of engagement* with the subjects we teach (see chart at right). When all life has been drained from a subject, we're back to desperately trying to motivate kids with tests, grades, stickers, and pizza.

The Engagement Continuum
(Saxton & Morgan, 1994)

Interest: being curious about a problem or topic

Engagement: wanting and striving to be involved in the tasks associated with the problem

Commitment: developing a sense of responsibility to the task and its importance; wanting to understand and adhere to community and disciplinary norms

Interpretation/Internalization: explaining, interpreting, and merging objective concepts (the content and processes to be learned to complete important tasks) with subjective experiences (what is already known, felt, and believed), resulting in deepened understanding and new insights and abilities

Application: finding new situations where the new understandings can be used

Generation: generating new data and interpretations that build on established sets of information

Communication: wanting to represent and communicate new understandings and questions to others

Evaluation: willingness to critique and refine understandings, and one's own learning process

Talk the Talk, Walk the Walk

If we're using kids' desire to be a member of the club in order to engage them, we must think about what it means to be a member of the club of historians, scientists, or mathematicians. We should be teaching them how to speak Math and how to *do* math. So we need to ask what kinds of texts mathematicians (or historians, or scientists) read and what concepts, strategies, and questions they use to read and write these texts and solve their problems. What do we need to do and know to be qualified members of the club? These issues are rarely pursued in school. They relate to the concerns I've previously expressed that we underarticulate the complexity of reading—particularly in the disciplines—and therefore fail to assist students in meeting the textual and disciplinary demands they are faced with as they progress through school.

"Inquiry puts students in touch with the original works and with the actual activity of practitioners. That is why it is exciting, and that is also why it works."

Now let's look at how the questioning schemes we reviewed in the previous chapters can be helpful in organizing disciplinary inquiry and in prompting disciplinary thinking.

QAR and Math

QAR works with any discipline. It can easily be adapted for use in math, science, and social sciences since these fields deal with problems, data, and representation in similar ways. Both the historian and the mathematician, for instance, ask what is already known, what patterns can be found in the data, what gaps need to be filled, and how to best (visually or verbally) represent the data to others.

During a brainstorming session with our national demo-site math teachers, they came up with this list of the ways that the scheme promotes mathematical thinking and decision making.

- **Right there** questions help students establish the facts and understand the details from the data/text, and identify unnecessary information/distractors.

- **Think and search** questions help students discern patterns and relationships in the data, and infer proper operations necessary to solve the problem.

- **Author and me** questions help students consider how to find missing information that might be helpful: identify a meaningful context in which solving this kind of problem would be useful in their lives; identify and apply proper operations; consider alternative operations and ways of solving the problem, as well as the costs and benefits, efficiencies and inefficiencies of each; check their work; evaluate the effectiveness of their procedures; hypothesize and articulate general principles; test hypotheses; and foreground decision making and meaning construction.
- **On my own** questions help students consider real-world applications of general principles and problem-solving procedures, identify situations in which concepts and strategies can be used, and think like mathematicians in their daily lives.

Too often math, as it's taught in schools, focuses on the "right answer," rather than on mathematical thinking and real-world situations. Among the greatest recommendations for using the QAR scheme with math is that it encourages a personal connection to the problem, reflection upon one's problem-solving processes, and a connection to issues in the world that the problem and strategies can help to address. In other words, students are moved along the continuum of engagement and competence! When students complain about math or struggle with it (or any other subject), it is usually because the activities they are given don't achieve these ends.

In a wonderful presentation on content-area literacy, Kay Haas Bushman offered these examples of math QARs offered on page 156.

QAR and Science

Dug Pusey is an extraordinary middle school science teacher who makes use of QAR in all of his units. For example, he began the school year with the inquiry *What would cause another ice age?*

The students engaged with several current news articles that presented various arguments on the relationship between the increase in carbon dioxide in the atmosphere and global warming. Dug points out that students must first understand the "right there" data in order to answer the subquestion *How does the atmosphere behave?* The students also explored the importance of other gases in the atmosphere, and the natural fluctuations in climatic changes over time due to a variety of factors. The students then had to "think and search" within

Problem	Right There	Think and Search	Author and Me	On My Own
A cord of seasoned almond wood costs $190. I paid $190 for a pile that was 4 feet wide, 2 feet high, and 10 feet long. Did I get an honest deal? (Cord—a rectangular pile of wood 4 feet high, 4 feet wide and 8 feet long.)	What is a cord? How much did I pay? How much does a cord of seasoned almond wood cost? What are the dimensions of the pile of wood I bought?	What five pieces of information do I need to solve this problem? What proportion of a cord does my pile of wood represent? What might be a reasonable price for the wood I actually received?	Would I purchase wood from this person again? How does the volume of wood I purchased compare with a cord? How could I attempt to estimate whether I really receive a cord in the future?	What would someone do with a cord of wood? Why is wood sold by the cord? Why does the type of wood matter when determining the cost?
A DVD store owner buys some DVDs to sell for $12 each. He then marks up the price of the DVDs by 20 percent. Not many sell at this price, so he marks the DVDs down 20 percent from the marked-up price. At the marked-down price, will the owner make a profit from the sale of the remaining DVDs?	What is the first thing the owner does to the price of the DVDs? When DVDs don't sell, what does the owner do?	What information is not needed? What was the original marked-up price on the DVDs? What was the final price after the markdown?	Determine the markdowns that would result in either a clear profit or a clear loss. What various strategies could you use to solve this problem and what are the costs and benefits of each? What is important to know about the selling price of DVDs?	How does a store owner determine the amount of markup for a product? What does a product's cost depend on (product, availability, supply and demand, etc.)? How do store owners survive when they sometimes must sell at a loss?

and across articles to look for various explanatory patterns. They then began to use what they had learned to stake claims of their own of what might happen in particular future situations (author and me) and to consider future applications of the general principles they had developed and the tools they had used (on my own).

Dug told me that the QARs were eminently useful in apprenticing the students into scientific thinking because they required the following processes:

- **Right there** questions promote careful observation and the consideration of direct evidence.
- **Think and search** questions promote the ability to see relationships among data and patterns across data sets, make reasonable inferences

and hypotheses, and consider indirect evidence to make predictions and theories.

Modeling Scientific Thinking

Let's take a look at how Dug used QAR in action to encourage these scientific turns of mind. In a unit on seismology, organized around the question *How will earthquakes affect our future?* Dug planned backwards from a culminating project in which students would provide a seismological analysis predicting future earthquake activity in their hometown (the subject of their topical research) and then provide another analysis for a different place where they had family or would like to live (their critical inquiry).

Dug had already completed frontloading about seismology. In this first of several news articles they would read, he helped students identify "right there" information, but he did so in service of reaching a much deeper level of engagement and understanding. (Note: In seismic studies, eyewitness accounts have been an important tool for estimating the size of an earthquake. Prior to having seismic stations around the world, newspaper accounts often provided sufficient information to at least approximately assess an earthquake's intensity.)

Dug: Students, today we get to go back in time . . . over a hundred years. We are going back to the largest earthquake in Utah in modern times. We will read the words of Mr. James Long and remind ourselves that we live near faults that will move again. In pairs, identify the key details offered in the account that will help us evaluate the intensity of the 1901 Central Utah Earthquake.

Poker Players Prayed

Earthquake in Southern Utah scared them

Threw hands into the deck and sent up earnest supplication—
then resumed the game

James Long, superintendent of the June Bug group of mining properties in the Gold mountain country, is in Salt Lake. Mr. Long was at Kimberley a few days ago when the earthquake occurred. "That was the real center of the disturbance," he said yesterday, "and it was no laughing matter, either. The first and severest shock was at 9:30 in the evening, and there were a number of smaller ones during the night. It was a regular upheaval, and had the houses been of brick they could not have stood. I was playing hearts with two others in the back room of a saloon at the time. The game was adjourned and we all ran out. I admit I ran, and I ran hard. I would have run farther, but I did not know where to run to. I am told on good authority that four men were engaged in a poker game at the time at Monroe, and that the meeting was at once resolved into the most enthusiastic prayer meeting ever held in Southern Utah. Later they resumed the game."

(*Salt Lake Tribune*, November 18, 1901)

Dug: Okay, let's hit what's right there: Mr. Long had come to Salt Lake City and reported his account to the newspaper. But in what town did he report that he experienced the earthquake?

Student 1: It says that the poker game was in Monroe. But Mr. Long was in Kimberly.

Dug: Right. Why might this be important?

Student 2: Might it be the epicenter? Or somewhere between Kimberly and Monroe?

Dug: It's certainly near it. Why might that be key? We're on to think and search now.

Student 1: You could predict the intensity of the earthquake at other places?

Dug: Right! Now let's keep doing think and search. How do the key details about the effects of the earthquake help us estimate its intensity?

Student 2: Hah! Those poker players got pretty shaken up 'cause they said they started praying.

Student 3: Yeah, and Mr. Long ran out like a scared cat!

Student 4: He said that if houses were made of brick, then they would have all come down.

Dug: Yes, but how do these various details work together to indicate intensity?

(Conversation continues around this theme, with students providing uptake for one another's comments.)

Dug: Okay, let's think about this with an "author and me" question to help us fill gaps. What tells you that this might not have been the most severe earthquake on the scale?

Student 5: Maybe what it doesn't say—nobody died.

Student 6: And they went back to their poker game. They were shaken up, but the wooden saloon wasn't broken up bad enough to stop their game.

Student 2: I wouldn't go back and play poker if I was really, really scared.

Dug: How would experiencing a similar earthquake affect you? *(Students discuss.)*

Dug: Okay, here is an "on your own" question. Looking at the high mountains that we live next to and the fault-line map, what should we do to prepare for the earthquakes that will definitely occur in our lifetimes?

(Conversation continues about ways of predicting earthquakes, developing new technologies, improving buildings, keeping a 72-hour kit, etc.)

Dug makes sure that key details are recognized by the students and then uses this to launch students into large and small groups, in which they do the work of seeing connections and their implications. Notice how organizing a class discussion around QARs yields a dialogic conversation that moves kids from topical research to critical inquiry and application. Such discussions can be produced with the other schemes as well. They are effective tools for forging powerful disciplinary discussions.

QARs can also be effective for reinforcing the habits of mind of a social scientist. A historian, for instance, would certainly ask what was already known, what patterns existed in the extant data, how to fill gaps, what it would be like to experience certain events, how to visually or dramatically represent historical situations to others, etc.

Questioning Circles and Science

Students in every school in America are constantly asking, "Why do we have to learn this stuff?" and "When are we ever going to use this?" The Questioning Circle immediately addresses such questions. Sixth-grade science teacher Denise Churchill—like many of our teachers—has found that using the circle to frame discussion enlivens student engagement with normally deadly textbook chapters. It connects them personally, as a disciplinary "novice expert," to what really matters in the material.

As part of her class's inquiry *What is healthy teen living?* (which culminated with a project on how their own behavior patterns such as diet and sleep affect their health), Denise used a questioning circle to review a science textbook chapter entitled "Simple Organisms and Viruses."

Pure Questions

- **Me**: What diseases have you had that were caused by viruses? How did you catch the virus? What kind of medical treatment did you receive? How effective were the treatments?

- **Text**: What are the parts of the immune system and how do they work together to fight a virus? What happens when a virus enters your body? Can a virus be medically treated?
- **World**: What other diseases have you heard of that are caused by viruses? What kind of impact have these diseases had on history? What kind of viral infections threaten the world today?

Shaded Questions

- **Me and text:** What vaccinations have you had? When did you get vaccinated? Why was it important for you to be vaccinated?
- **Me and world**: Do you face the same risk from viral diseases as adolescents did 50 years ago? 100 years ago? Why or why not?
- **Text and world**: What impact did the smallpox virus have on Native Americans? What impact has the HIV virus had on people today? What effect might future viruses have?

Dense Questions (Me/Text/World)

- Given what we know from the text and history, do you think children should be required to be vaccinated for certain diseases before starting school? Why or why not?
- Given what we know from the text and history, should people diagnosed with a deadly virus like HIV be quarantined from others? Should they be allowed to attend school? Why or why not?

Denise wrote afterward: "I was really impressed by the thoughtfulness in student responses. We started out with the pure questions—they really liked talking about themselves and what experiences they had had with viruses. All but three had had chicken pox, and we had to stop and share scars!! All students were engaged in the discussion. I wish it had been a smaller group—there were a lot of kids, and they all wanted to share. I will put kids in smaller groups next time. We ended up using two and a half class periods to complete our discussion. But it actually worked well that way, because the first break allowed them to check on their own immunization records and the second break gave them time to think about answers to the dense questions. We all pretty much agreed with the need for required vaccinations, but the quarantine question was really split. I felt the kids did a great job of listening to each other and defending their own beliefs. I liked this questioning approach much better than any other questioning scheme I've used before. It was more engaging to students. It also gave them a personal relationship to the material as it showed them how it was connected to real-world issues. I think it really helped them think like scientists and see scientific kinds of insights. It led to great discussion that was based on scientific concepts and ideas. I'll definitely use it again—soon."

Reviewing Whole Units With a Questioning Scheme

Each of these schemes can also work well to organize a review of an entire unit.

When I team-teach social studies, I often use the questioning circle as a way to review the unit and prep students for their final projects. I recently did so during a civil rights unit, planning backwards from the creation of video documentaries that addressed the question *What can you do to protect and promote civil rights?* In the videos, the students would review the historical trends of a civil rights issue that interested them and then propose a course of future action.

After a discussion using the following questioning circle, my teaching partner Paul Friedemann had this to say: "They're ready for anything now, aren't they? They nailed this stuff as citizens, as students, and as social scientists. If they can answer all those questions then they are ready to take a test, argue a position, make the video, whatever. They *know* this stuff—and they know it the way we want students to know something. They know what they know and they know how and why they know it!"

Paul was saying that the circle succeeded in promoting our students' engagement and disciplinary understanding as social scientists. And that was the point and purpose of our class.

Rethinking "Coverage" and Textbooks

The teachers with whom I work seem to grasp intuitively the power of the inquiry approach, but they often resist because, as they say, "I just don't have the time—there's so much content to cover!" Wiggins and McTighe (1998) argue that this kind of statement confuses information and knowledge, and confuses superficial coverage with the "uncoverage" of true understanding of

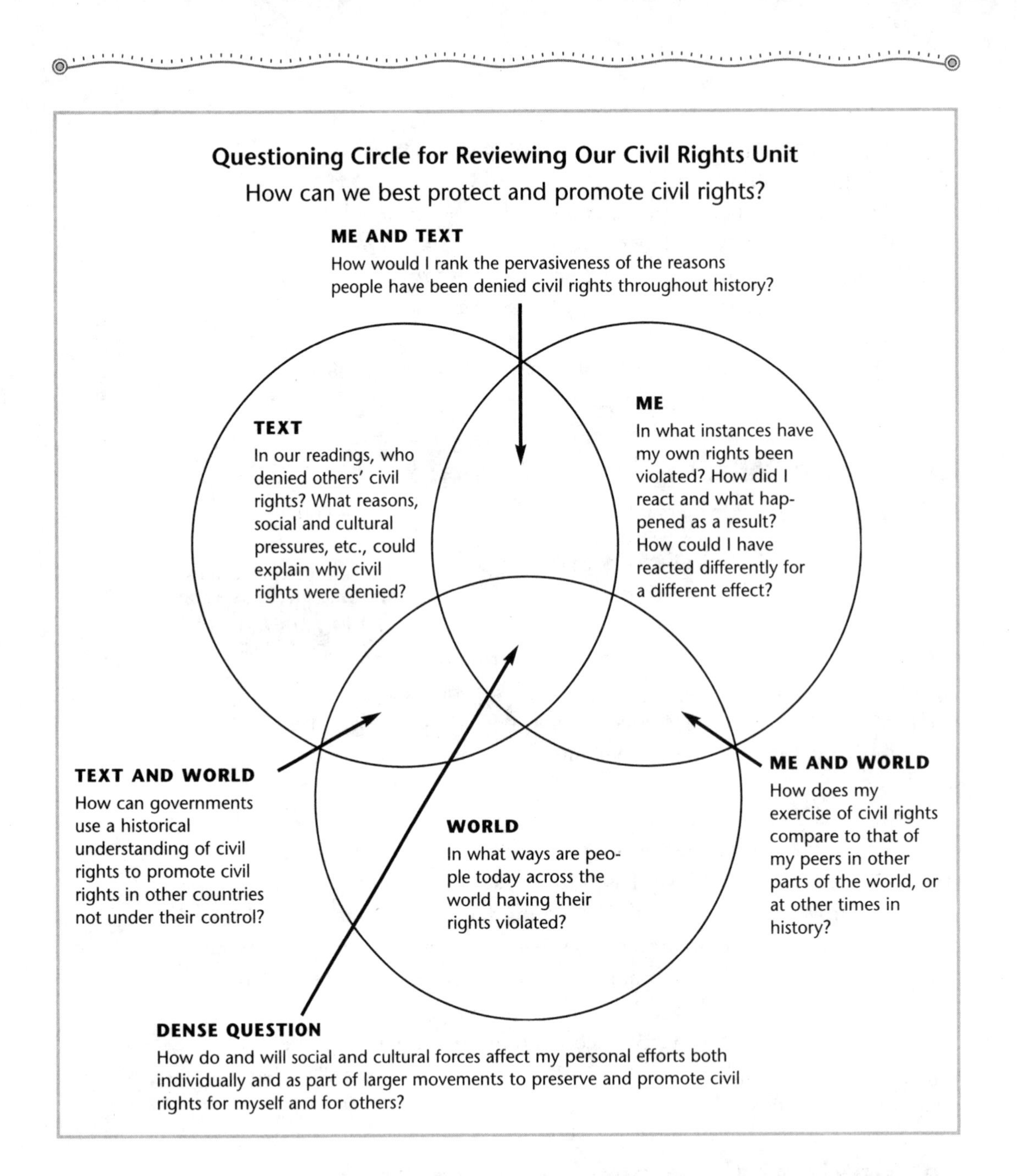

how data is structured, and how and why knowledge structures work. These researchers show how the "coverer"—the teacher—acts with the belief that textbooks and tests are the best way to promote understanding and the ability to use the material. Much research shows, however, that relying on a textbook does not yield the gains that inquiry-oriented teaching does. To take just one example, the Third International Mathematics and Science Study, or TIMSS,

(2003) reported that inquiry leads to more engagement, retention, understanding, application—and higher test scores. Other studies by the Whirlwind and Annenberg projects found in Chicago's schools also found that even short inquiry treatments had many positive effects on motivation, interaction, achievement—and test scores (A-E-P, 2002; Rose, Parks, Androes, & McMahon, 2000).

The Textbook as One of Many Tools

Inquiry contexts change how the textbook is used. No longer is it a sacred text, the embodiment of the curriculum. In inquiry, it becomes just one resource that provides a summation from the dominant viewpoint. The class calls upon other texts and resources, including student activities and prior experience. Many national commissions and studies have called for less reliance on textbooks and more use of primary documents, hands-on learning experiences, and inquiry orientations. Ernest Boyer's Carnegie Commission report (1983) said this: "Most textbooks present students with a highly simplified view of reality and practically no insight into the methods by which the information has been gathered and the facts distilled. Moreover, textbooks seldom communicate to students the richness and excitement of the original works" (p. 143).

Concluding Thoughts: On Motivation and Deep Understanding

The teacher's job is to promote learning and understanding. Inquiry—with its use of guiding questions, meaning-constructive discussions, local-level questions, and questioning schemes for navigating texts and data sets—does just that. It promotes the sort of deep understanding held by experts in the field.

But first, students have to be motivated.

When Michael Smith and I studied the literacy lives of boys, we found that they were willing to engage in any activity that met certain conditions—what the psychologist Csikszentmihalyi (1990) calls the conditions of "flow." According to Csikszentmihalyi, flow exists when there is a sense of control and competence, a challenge that requires an appropriate level of skill, clear goals and feedback, and a focus on the immediate experience. These four conditions, plus one that we added—the importance of the social aspects—resounded in our data on whether boys engaged or disengaged with a particular activity (See Smith & Wilhelm, 2002, 2006).

Inquiry meets all the conditions of flow. Every activity in this book, appropriately used, meets all these conditions. Inquiry can foster flow and engagement in your classroom on a daily basis! The student-centered approach doesn't provide some aspects of the social or the appropriate challenge; the information-transmission approach meets none of the conditions. Is it any wonder that students often look dazed and doze off in such classes?

John Guthrie, one of our foremost researchers on motivation, has shown in his work that motivating and engaging classrooms are:

Observational

- They provide interactions with the real world.
- Observing the world is a departure point for extended literacy and learning; everything is connected to real-world problems and practices.

Conceptual

- There is a focus on deep understanding of what is observed, of explanatory and foundational ideas.
- Students actively inquire to find answers/solutions.
- Inquiry leads to explanation and action.
- Students achieve in-depth understanding.
- Students learn many things through one thing.

Self-Directed

- Study leads to self-directed, independent learning (i.e., critical inquiry).
- There is a sequence of support for growing autonomy.
- Students participate in decision making and meaning making.

Strategic

- There is explicit support for problem-solving and understanding provided when it's needed and provided over time.
- All strategies are learned in order to do work, to achieve immediate functional ends.
- All strategies are learned in a situation where they can be applied.

Collaborative

- There is a social construction of ideas; students work with the teacher, one another, and with experts (either directly or through texts).

- There is a sense of belonging to a community of practice.
- There is a sharing and social use for what is learned.

Coherent

- Learning experiences are sequenced and connected, and work together to build toward deep understanding and action.

Personalized

- Students construct and represent their own disciplinary understandings.
- Students are able to use a discipline's concepts and language to express and justify their own claims about issues of importance.

(Guthrie, 2002; Guthrie & Anderson, 1999)

Once again, we can see that the inquiry approach provides all of the characteristics of a classroom that motivates and engages students. And it is these same characteristics that produce meaningful interactions with the material that promote deep understanding.

Since what we teach really does matter, why not teach it in such a way that students can share your excitement and your understanding of how and why learning it is important, for their lives today and in the future? The strongest recommendation for an inquiry approach is that it motivates students, which in turn leads them to engage with seminal concepts and strategies, which in turn can be used as tools for achieving true understanding. I hope this book helps you to use inquiry and the tools of dialogue and student questioning in just such ways. There is no question about one thing: inquiry works, and it works because it meets our basic human need for what we do to matter. It helps satisfy our need to become more competent and independent in ways that count in the world.

What we want for our students is for them to be able to participate in disciplinary conversations, either as members of a community of practice or tangentially, as democratic citizens weighing in on the issues that affect us all. After all, as John Dewey maintained, democracy is conversation. Using questions and dialogue to make meaning helps us pursue both understanding *and* democracy, and both are ends worth working toward.

ACKNOWLEDGMENTS

It's humbling during a project such as writing this book to try to tease out one's teachers and trace the provenance of one's ideas. This book would have been impossible to write without the bloodlines and inspiration provided by many people:

Rich Lehrer, who introduced me to inquiry and design when I was a doctoral student at the University of Wisconsin; Paul Friedemann, who helped me develop inquiry-driven curricula; Brian Ambrosius, an ever-helpful colleague; Grant Wiggins and Jay McTighe who furthered my thinking about inquiry through their work with understanding by design; George Hillocks whose seminal work in teaching language arts and personal generosity are tremendous; and thanks to George's students–Tom McCann, Peter Smagorinsky, Larry Johannessen, Elizabeth Kahn, and many others—for their assistance helping me think about the role of questions and discussion to develop understanding.

Thanks to my colleagues at the University of Maine who supported my work with the national demonstration site in adolescent literacy across the content areas project in Washington County, Maine. This is where many of the ideas in these pages were worked out and tested. Thank you as well to Myra Tollestrup and the BYU/CITES network for allowing me to continue my inquiry work with them through a national dissemination site. Special thanks to Dug Pusey, Scott Hendrickson, Tammy King and all the content area leaders from this project.

I am deeply grateful to the fabulous teachers at West Junior High School (especially Marian Workman, Yvonne Georgeson, Ruthanne Beddoe, et al), and at Foothills School of Arts and Sciences for allowing me to work in their classrooms.

On the personal side, a 31 gun salute to all my friends, colleagues, and my family: Peggy Jo, Fiona Luray and Jasmine Marie for all of their support. My thanks also to the Foster-Sears family, with whom we spent 10 days in Mexico as I completed the first draft of this book. Thanks to Pierre DuMont for his seaside get-away in Maine where I completed the third draft.

Bushels of gratitude to my patient, indulgent and very appreciated Scholastic editors, Anne Trubek and Wendy Murray.

And I couldn't have done it without my colleagues and friends in the Boise State Writing Project, Maine Writing Project and the National Writing Project, where so many of the best teaching ideas take shape and are shared.

Thank you, thank you, and a googleplex of mega-thank yous to Tanya Baker, who has helped with every step of my inquiry journey, and to Michael W. Smith, who has helped with every step of my teaching and research journey.

BIBLIOGRAPHY

Applebee, A. N. (1996). *Curriculum as conversation: Transforming traditions of teaching and learning.* Chicago: University of Chicago Press.

Applebee, A. N., Burroughs, R., & Stevens, A.S. (2000). Shaping conversations: A study of continuity and coherence in high school literature curricula. *Research in the Teaching of English,* 34, 396-429.

Applebee, A.N., Langer, J., Nystrand, M., and Gamoran, A. (2003). Discussion-based approaches to developing understanding: Classroom instruction and student performance in middle and high school English, *American Educational Research Journal,* Fall.

Art Education Partnership (2002). Critical links: Learning in the arts and student academic and social development. Washington D.C.: Arts Education Partnership www.aep-arts.org

Bakhtin, M./Medvedev (1986). Speech genres and other late essays. V. W. McGee Trans. C. Emerson and M. Holquist, Eds. Austin, TX: University of Texas Press.

Beck, C. and Kosnick, C. (2004).The starting point: Constructivist accounts of learning. In *Teaching for Deep Understanding* (p. 13-20.) Toronto, ONT: OISE/EFTO.

Beck, I. L. and McKeown, M.G. (2002). Questioning the Author: Making Sense of Social Studies. *Educational Leadership* (60)3, 44-47.

Beck and McKeown (2006). *Improving Comprehension with Questioning the Author.* New York: Scholastic.

Beck, I.L., McKeown, M.G., Hamilton, R., Kucan, L. (1997). *Questioning the Author: An approach for enhancing student engagement with text.* Newark, DE: International Reading Association.

Bereiter, C. (2004). Reflections on depth. In *Teaching for Deep Understanding* (p. 8-12.) Toronto, ONT: OISE/UT and EFTO

Bloom, B. (1976). *Human characteristics and school learning.* New York: McGraw-Hill.

Booth, W. (1983). *The Company We Keep: Ethics of Fiction.*

Boyer, E. (1985). *High school: A report on secondary education in America.* New York: HarperCollins.

Brandt, D. (2001). *Literacy in American lives.* New York: Cambridge University Press.

Brown, J., Collins, A., and Duguid, P. (1989). Situated cognition and the culture of learning. *Educational Researcher* (18) 32-42.

Bulman, L. (1985). *Teaching language and study skills in secondary science* (pp. 110-111). London: Heinemann.

Cambourne, B. (1995).Toward an educationally relevant theory of literacy learning: Twenty years of inquiry. *The Reading Teacher, 49(3),* 182-190.

Cambourne, B. (2002). Conditions for Literacy Learning: The conditions of learning: Is learning natural? *The Reading Teacher* 55(8), 758-762.

Collins, A., Brown, J., & Newman, S. (1992). Cognitive apprenticeship: Teaching the crafts of reading, writing, and mathematics. In L. B. Resnick (Ed.) *Knowing, learning and instruction: Essays in honor of Robert Glaser.* (pp. 453-494). Hillsdale, NJ: Lawrence Erlbaum.

Cristoph, J. N. and Nystrand, M. (2001). Taking risks, negotiating relationships: One teacher's transition. *Research in the teaching of English.* 36, 2 (November): 249-286.

Csikszentmihalyi, M. (1990). *Flow: The Psychology of Optimal Experience.* New York: HarperCollins.

Delpit, (1995). *Other People's Children: Cultural Conflict in the Classroom.* New York: New York Press.

Dewey, J. (1916). *Democracy in Education.* New York: Basic Books.

Dillon, J.T. (1988a). Teaching and Questioning: a manual of practice. London: Croom Helm.

Dillon, J. T. (1988b). Questioning and Discussion: A multidisciplinary study. Norwood, NJ: Ablex.

Dysktra, D. (2006). talk at Idaho State Legislature, Education Committee of the House, April 3, 2006. www.ipn.uni-kiel.de/aktuell/stcse/stcse.html

Gee, J. (2003). *What Video Games Have to Teach Us About Learning and Literacy.* New York. Palgrave-Macmillan.

Edwards, A. and Westgate, D. (1987). *Investigating classroom talk.* London: Falmer Press.

Evans, K. (2002). Fifth-grade students' perceptions of how they experience literature discussion groups. *Reading Research Quarterly* (37)1, 46-69.

Erikson, E. (1963). *Childhood and society* (2nd edition). New York: Norton.

Freire, P., & Macedo, D. (1987). *Literacy: Reading the word & the world.* Westport, CT: Bergin & Garvey.

Gee, J. (2003). *What video games have to teach us about learning and literacy.* New York: Palgrave-Macmillan.

Goodlad, J. (2003). A nation in wait. *Education Week, 22, 32* (April 23).

Goodlad, J. (1984). *A place called school.* New York: McGraw-Hill.

Graves, D. (1983). *Writing: teachers and children at work.* Portsmouth, NH: Heinemann.

Guthrie, J.T., & Anderson, E. (1999). Engagement in reading: Processes of motivated, strategic, knowledgeable, social readers. In *Engaged reading: Processes, practices, and policy implications.* New York: Teachers College Press.

Guthrie, J. (2002). Classroom contexts for engaged reading: An overview, retrieved September 1, 2005 from www.cori.umd.edu/Research/Papers/Classroom.htm

Harvey, S., & Goudvis, A. (2000). *Strategies that work: Teaching comprehension to enhance understanding.* York, ME: Stenhouse.

Heathcote, D., & Bolton, G. (1995). *Drama for learning: Dorothy Heathcote's mantle of the expert approach for teaching drama.* Portsmouth, NH: Heinemann.

Hillocks , G. (1980). Towards a hierarchy of comprehension in literature. *English Journal*

Hillocks, G, Jr. (1986). The writer's knowledge: Theory, research and implications for practice. In D. Barthalomae and A Petrosky, Eds. *The Teaching of Writing, 85th Yearbook of the national society of the study of education* (pp. 71-94). Chicago: University of Chicago Press.

Hillocks, G., Jr., (1995). *Teaching writing as reflective practice.* New York: Teachers College Press.

Hillocks, G., Jr. (1999). *Ways of thinking, ways of teaching.* New York: Teachers College Press.

Hillocks, G. Jr. (2002). *The testing trap: How state writing assessments control learning.* New York: Teachers College Press.

Jacobs, H.H. (1989). *Interdisciplinary curriculum: Design and implementation.* Washington, DC: ASCD.

Jerry, L., and Lutkus, A. (2003). The nation's report card: Reading highlights from the NAEPs, 2002: 2002 Reading trends differ by grade. NCES 2003524.

Johannessen, L. R., Kahn, E. & Walter, C. C. (1982). *Designing and sequencing prewriting activities.* Urbana, IL: NCTE and ERIC.

Kahn, E., Walter, C., and Johannessen, L. (1984). Making small groups work: Controversy is key. *English Journal,* 73, 63-65.

Kirsch, I., Jungeblut, A., Jenkins, L., & Kolstad, A. (1993). Adult literacy in America: A first look at the findings of the National Adult Literacy Survey. Washington, D.C: National Center for Educational Statistics. Retrieved September 30, 2004, from nces.ed.gov/pubsearch/pubsinfo.asp?pubid=93275.

Lampert, M. (1990). When the problem is not the question and the solution is not the answer: Mathematical knowing and teaching. *American Educational Research Journal, 27* (1), 50-51.

Langer, J., A. (1993). Discussion as exploration: Literature and the horizon of possibilities. In G.E. Newell and R.K. Durst *Exploring texts: the role of discussion and writing in the teaching and learning of literature.* (pp. 23–44). Norwood, MA: Christopher Gordon Publishers.

Langer, J. A. (1995). *Envisioning literature: Literary understanding and literature instruction.* New York: Teachers College Press

Langer, J. A. (2001). Beating the odds: Teaching middle and high school students to read and write well. *American Educational Research Journal,* 38, 4: 837-880.

Lave, J. and Wenger, E. (1991). *Situated learning: Legitimate peripheral participation.* New York: Cambridge University Press.

Lee, C. (2001). Is October Brown Chinese? A cultural modeling activity system for underachieving students. American Educational Research Journal 38 (1) 97-141.

Manzo, A. V. (1969). The ReQuest procedure. *The Journal of Reading,* 13(2), 123-126.

Marshall, J. D. (1987). The effects of writing on students' understanding of literary texts. *Research in the Teaching of English,* 21, 30-63.

Marshall, J. D., Smagorinsky, P., & Smith, M. W. (1995). *The language of interpretation: Patterns of discourse in discussions of literature.* Urbana, IL: NCTE.

McCann, T., Johannessen, L., Kahn, E. Smagorinsky, P., and Smith, M.W. (2005). *Reflective teaching; reflective practice: How to develop critically engaged readers, writers, and speakers.* Portsmouth, NH: Heinemann.

McCann,T., Johannessen, L., Kahn, E., Flanagan, J. (2002). Let's Talk: Strategies for initiating and sustaining authentic discussion. NCTE Annual Convention, Atlanta, GA. November 24, 2002.

McCann, T.M., Flanagan, J.M., Johannessen, L.R., & Kahn, E. (2006). Talking in class. Using Discussion to Enhance Teaching and Learning. Urbana, IL: NCTE.

McTighe, J., Seif, E., and Wiggins, G. (2004). You can teach for meaning. *Phi Delta Kappan, 62*(1), 26-31.

Moore, G.E. (2003). Improving classroom presentation skills [electronic version] Retrieved from www.ais.msstate.edu/TALS/unit2/2moduleD.html retrieved September 1, 2005.

Morgan, N. and Saxton, J. (1994). *Asking better questions: models, techniques and classroom activities for engaging students in learning.* Markham, ONT: Pembroke Publishers, Ltd.

National Assessment of Student Progress (NAEP). (2003). *The nation's report card: Reading, 2002.* Washington, D.C.: U.S. Department of Education, Office of Educational Research and Improvement.

National Assessment of Student Progress (NAEP). (2005). The nation's report card: reading 2005. Washington, D.C.: U.S. Department of Education, Office of Educational Research and Improvement. Additional data retrieved May 3, 2006, from http://nces.ed.gov/nationsreportcard/nrc/reading math 2005/s0002.asp

National Endowment for the Arts (2004). *Reading at Risk: A survey of literary reading in America. Research Division Report #46.* Washington, D.C: NEA. For an electronic copy of the report, see www.arts.gov/news/news04/ReadingAtRisk.html

Nickerson, R.S. (1985). Understanding understanding. *American Journal of Education, 93,* 201-239.

Nystrand, M. and Gamoran, A. (1996). Student engagement: When recitation becomes conversation. In W. Waxman & H. Walberg (Eds.), *Contemporary Research on Teaching.*

Nystrand, M., with Gamoran, A., Kachur, R., & Prendergast, C. (1997). *Opening dialogue: Understanding the dynamics of language and learning in the English classroom.* New York: Teachers College Press.

Perkins, D. N. (1986). *Knowledge as Design.* Hillsdale, NJ: Erlbaum.

Rabinowitz, P., & Smith, M. W. (1998). *Authorizing readers: Resistance and respect in the teaching of literature.* New York: Teachers College Press.

Rand Reading Study Group. (2002). *Reading for understanding: Toward a R&D Program in Reading Comprehension.* Santa Monica, CA: RAND.

Raphael, T. (1982). Question answering strategies for children. *Reading Teacher* (36)2, 186-190.

Resnick, L. (1999, June 16). Making America smarter. Education week on the web [online] Accessed July 5, 1999. Available: ww.edweek.org/ew/1999/40resnick

Rogoff, B., Matusov, B., White, S. (1996). Models of teaching and learning: Participation in a community of learners. In D. Olson and N. Torrance, (Eds.) *The handbook of cognition and human development* (Pp. 388-414). Oxford, UK: Blackwell.

Rose, D.S., Parks, M., Androes, K., and McMahon, S.D. (2000, September). Imagery-based learning: Improving elementary students' reading comprehension with drama techniques. *Journal of Educational Research,* 94 (1), 55.

Ross, J.A., Hogaboam-Gray, A. & McDougall, B., & Le Sage, A. (2003). A survey measuring implementation of mathematics education reform by elementary teachers. *Journal of Research in Mathematics Education,* 34(4), 344-363.

Rowe, M. B. (2003). Wait-time and rewards as instructional variables, their influence on language, logic and fate control. *Journal of Research in Science Teaching* v 40(3), 19-32.

Sizer, T. (1984). Horace's Compromise. New York: Houghton-Mifflin.

Smagorinsky, P. and Fly, P.K. (1994). A new perspective on why small groups do and don't work. *English Journal,* 83, 3 (March) 54-58.

Smith, M. W., & Wilhelm. J. (2002). *"Reading don't fix no Chevys": Literacy in the lives of young men.* Portsmouth, NH: Heinemann.

Smith, M. and Wilhelm, J. (2006). *Going with the flow.* Portsmouth, NH: Heinemann.

Soder, R. (1999). *When words find their meaning: Renewal versus reform. Phi Delta Kappan.* April, 568-570.

Tharp, R. and Gallimore, R.(1988). *Rousing minds to life.* Cambridge, UK: Cambridge University Press.

Third International Math and Science Survey (2003). Institute for Education Statistics. Data retrieved September 1, 2005, from http://nces.ed.gov/timiss/September 1, 2005.

Travers, R. (1998). What is a good guiding question? *Educational Leadership* (*65*)6, 70-73.

Tyler, R. (1949). *Basic principles of curriculum and instruction.* Chicago: University of Chicago Press.

Weglinsky, H. (2004). Facts or critical thinking skills. *Phi Delta Kappan 62*(1), 32-35.

White, B. (1995). The effects of autobiographical writing before reading upon students' responses to short stories. *The Journal of Educational Research, 88,* 173-184.

Wieman, C. (2005). Physics by Inquiry. Speech given in Pueblo, CO, July 21, 2005.

Wiggins, G. and McTighe, J. (1998, 2003). *Understanding by Design.* Alexandria, VA: ASCD.

Wilhelm, J. (1997). *"You gotta BE the book": Teaching engaged and reflective reading with adolescents.* New York: Teachers College Press.

Wilhelm, J., and Friedemann, P. (1998). *Hyperlearning: Where inquiry, projects and technology meet.* York, ME: Stenhouse.

Wilhelm, Baker and Dube-Hackett, J. (2001). *Strategic Reading: Guiding the lifelong literacy of adolescents.* Portsmouth, NH: Heinemann.

Wilhelm, J. (2001). *Improving comprehension with think alouds.* New York: Scholastic.

Wilhelm, J. (2002). *Action strategies for deepening comprehension.* New York: Scholastic.

Wilhelm, J. (2004). *Reading IS seeing.* New York: Scholastic.

Wilson, E.O. (2004). The diversity of life. Distinguished Lecture. Boise State University, Boise, Idaho, April 14, 2004.

Zeichner, K. and Tabachik, B. (1981). Are the effects of university teacher education "washed out" by school experience? Journal of Teacher Education 32 (3) 7-11.

INDEX

R

S

T

U

W

X

Y

Z